D1391861

Mel Noakes is a certified life and health coach, NLP practitioner and hypnotherapist, who has won acclaim for her work as the Self Care Coach. She specialises in programmes tailored for women – online and in person – helping them to balance successful professional lives with health and happiness, and to start loving the skin, and life, they're in. To discover more, visit melnoakes.com.

the little book of
Self Care

the tiny everyday habits that will transform your life

Mel Noakes

EBURY
PRESS

1 3 5 7 9 10 8 6 4 2

Ebury Press, an imprint of Ebury Publishing
20 Vauxhall Bridge Road
London SW1V 2SA

Ebury Press is part of the Penguin Random House group of companies
whose addresses can be found at global.penguinrandomhouse.com

Penguin
Random House
UK

Designed and set by seagulls.net

Chapter opener illustrations © designer_an – Fotolia
All other illustrations © lakalla – Fotolia

First published by Ebury Press in 2017

www.penguin.co.uk

A CIP catalogue record for this book is available from the British Library

ISBN 9781785037313

Printed and bound in Great Britain by Clays Ltd, St Ives PLC

MIX
Paper from
responsible sources
FSC® C018179

Penguin Random House is committed to a
sustainable future for our business, our readers
and our planet. This book is made from Forest
Stewardship Council® certified paper.

To Olivia, Megan, Max, Seb and
Baby Noakes, who we can't wait to meet.
I hope self care will be something your
generation never have to struggle with.

contents

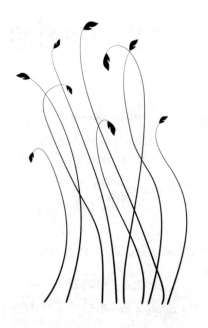

introduction

I was an ambitious and adventurous woman who appeared to have a life most people dream of. A great job, I travelled a lot and was always with friends and at events.

From the outside, it appeared as if I had it all, but secretly I thought. 'If they only knew.' Despite the trappings of success I had battled with an eating disorder and low self-esteem for most of my teens and twenties. A good day was characterised by what I ate or didn't eat, how much I exercised and how hard I pushed myself. I was so far down my list of priorities that nothing could make up for a fundamental lack of self care. My life looked great on paper but felt like crap in real life.

They say 'you teach what you most need to learn'. Self care has been my biggest teacher and lesson. From my late twenties I had to relearn new habits and learn to love and respect myself, not something I found easy. Daily acts of kindness grew into something more profound, and slowly I realised how nourishing myself enabled me to live a much fuller, happier and extraordinary life.

After almost fifteen years of therapy and much soul searching, I took a year long trip to Latin America that changed my life. At the end of a four-day Inca hike to Machu Picchu, I finally had the breakthrough I needed. As I stood at the sun gate, I was humbled and amazed to be there. In all the years I'd fought my body, hated it, starved it and battled with it, it had never given up. My body had fought back and it had allowed me the privilege of doing something as amazing as the Inca hike, when all the stats said I shouldn't even be alive.

In that moment I made peace with myself and my body. I decided to start living my life rather than just existing... And now I help other people do the same.

Life is a gift – an adventure, a series of experiences, opportunities and lessons.

To truly live it, we need to correctly fuel our body, mind and soul. We need to discover self care.

This book is designed specifically to give you inspiration and ideas to open you up to new possibilities and choices. Feeling stuck or helpless happens when we feel we don't have anywhere to go and when our choices are limited. This book is your go to guide, your pocket inspiration and your opportunity to see life, your life, through a different lens and see you always have a choice.

You don't need to integrate all the tips into your life, but what you'll find is when you truly practise self care, many of these tips naturally become part of your daily routine. I recommend dipping in and out when you need it, trying the tips that feel the most fun, relevant or valuable to you in that moment and when you find tips that work for you, committing to integrate them into your regular self-care practice.

book bonuses

Visit melnoakes.com/book to claim your free bonuses, including cheat sheets, worksheets, how to guides and lots of other useful stuff. You'll find many of the worksheets and ideas shared in this book available on the site for you to download and use as you work through the book.

what is self care and why should you care?

Self care is the actions we undertake to look after ourselves: physically, emotionally and mentally.

Let me ask you a question – Do you nourish yourself or punish yourself?

Take a minute, digest the question and answer truthfully.

For many of us, the truth is, we punish ourselves more frequently than perhaps we realise. In our heads, we berate ourselves for missing a deadline, or saying the wrong thing or appearing stupid. We don't dress well because we feel clothes are frivolous or our bodies are unworthy. We put ourselves last and others first because we want to be liked and accepted. We go to the gym to run off the food we feel guilty about eating the day before. We work late to prove ourselves to our boss, colleagues and ourselves. We don't take holidays. We create busyness to justify our importance and make us feel valued. We cram so many things into our diary to feel we're living that we don't have time to sleep.

We put pressure on ourselves to be perfect and expect nothing less, yet accept far less from others.

It's no wonder so many of us are burnt out, worn out, exhausted and confused.

My friend, this is punishment.

Let's look at the flip side. Believing you're capable and able to do anything you put your mind to. Acknowledging the good in you and your life. Surrounding yourself with people that love and champion you. Going to the gym or for a run because it makes your body feel amazing and strong, and because you want to be able to live healthily. Choosing to eat food that makes you feel good and gives you energy, as well as being able to enjoy indulgent food without feeling guilty. Taking time out to recharge, rest and restore, so you can be fully present in the moments that matter and spend quality time with the people you love. Making a difference in the world and choosing to give time to things and people that matter. Creating an environment around you that feels safe, calm and relaxing. Allowing people to love you because you love yourself.

This my friend is nourishment and radical self care.

Let's look at the science.

Stress is your body's natural way to respond to danger. If you are consistently experiencing stress then it can play havoc in your body. Chronic stress disrupts nearly every system in your body. It can suppress your immune system, increase the risk of heart attack and stroke, upset your digestive and reproductive systems, and speeds up the aging process.

It can even rewire your brain, leaving you more vulnerable to anxiety, depression and other mental health problems.

Regular self care practice has been shown to lower stress levels and improve health. It is one of the most positive things you can do for yourself.

Health and wellbeing isn't elitist. You don't need to join a fancy gym, shop in specialist stores, buy expensive gear, drink expensive juices or buy expensive detoxes. Whilst those things are great, if you can afford them, they're not pre-requisite for your health or self care.

This book is filled with tips and ideas that you'll probably think are really simple and easy.

That's exactly the point.

Self care isn't rocket science.

Often the most profound things in life are the simple, everyday things we know but somehow think are irrelevant because, well, life is meant to be hard isn't it?

No, it's not.

Here's to the journey. Your journey.

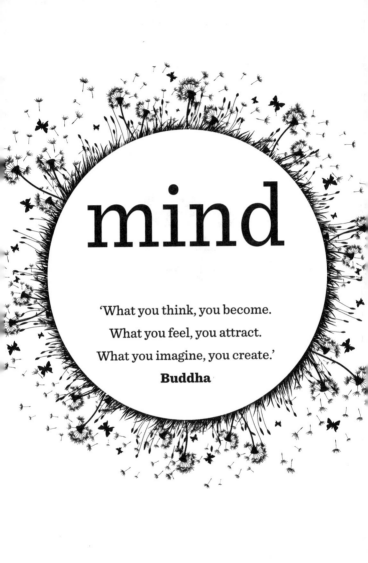

mind

'What you think, you become.
What you feel, you attract.
What you imagine, you create.'
Buddha

The foundations of wellbeing, self care and how we live and feel about our lives all start with our minds. What we think impacts the way we feel about things, and this in turn affects our actions. So, whenever we discuss wellbeing, we need to start with what's going on in our thoughts.

Looking after ourselves and feeling we're deserving of attention and care are the keys to wellbeing. Believing, fundamentally, we are worthy of good things means we treat ourselves with respect. We nourish our bodies with healthy nutritious food and we move our bodies because it feels good to do so – not to punish ourselves for some perceived 'sin' or to maintain a certain body shape. We surround ourselves with healthy relationships. We invest in our personal growth and we flourish.

Like so many others, I've experienced the other side of this coin, whereby we believe we're not good enough; where we need to be perfect to be loved and accepted; where we feel we're somehow 'bad', and the only way to change is to be harsh on ourselves and constantly push ourselves to prove we're worthy of affection and love.

We all have bad days, moments when we say or do something we regret, and periods of time when, perhaps, life isn't going according to plan and we'd rather just stay in bed. And it's true that life is often challenging and bad things happen. People die; relationships fail; we don't always get the job, the person or the house of our dreams. Our finances aren't always stable. People we love get sick. We witness injustices. This is all part and parcel of the real world. Self care is not about how full the glass is or ignoring the realities of life; it's about learning to accept the glass and life as it is.

When you have positive self-regard, or self-love, you will have more resilience and the ability to cope with life's unexpected turns because you're able to draw on your internal strengths. You won't beat yourself up over every bad thing that happens, but equally you won't need to shirk the blame if you ought to accept some responsibility. Your view of yourself will be truly balanced and not reliant on external sources for validation.

This part of the book is designed to help you improve the way you perceive yourself and the world around you. It's designed to help you question the stories you tell yourself about who you are and the nature of the world. It aims to help you become curious and compassionate and to learn to love yourself from the inside out.

let's talk about mental health

Nearly two thirds of the UK population have experienced a mental health problem at some point in their lifetime while, in the USA, one in five adults suffer from a mental health condition (that's more than the population of New York and Florida combined!). All around the world, mental health issues impact people of every background and social status, whether they are male or female, young or old, black or white, rich or poor.

So let's discuss the elephant in the room. Looking after our mental health is fundamental to our self care. Our minds are complicated and intricate, and coping with the pressures of modern day life can sometimes create issues that require specialist help. However, when you've lived in the fog of a mental health issue for a long time, it can be hard to understand that this is not a 'normal' way of living, as you come to accept the way you feel. While it can be hard to admit that things aren't perfect and Instagram worthy, when it comes to mental health often the only way things can start to improve is when you actively step forward and ask for professional support. At the back of this book, on page 195 of the Self Care Toolkit, you'll find a list of organisations that can assist you. If you suspect you might be suffering with your own mental health, I would encourage you to take that first step, as living with mental health disorders can be vastly improved and even entirely resolved with the right help.

storytelling

The human brain is constantly active, regulating the body, sending messages to the limbs to perform actions, processing data from the senses, sending messages and pulling up memories to help us interact effectively with the world around us. The fact that brain activity consumes some 20 per cent of our calorie intake each day gives a sense of how powerful the brain is.

So, what happens in our brains when we're processing information? In a nutshell, the brain tries to make things simple for us. The brain is like a massive filing system storing memories and information, which it does by filtering data so we retain only what is most valuable. It goes about this in three ways: it deletes information that isn't relevant; it generalises or makes data fit existing patterns that make sense to us; or it distorts data to meet certain assumptions and beliefs we already hold.

So the memories we store in our heads are our own *personalised* version of events, subject to how our brain has interpreted them. Take the example of going to a party with a friend. You both attend the same party but when you get home and compare your stories about the night, you both have slightly different versions. You were both at exactly the same event, yet you captured the information differently.

This happens throughout our lives. We form our own picture of who we are, as well as of the world and our place in it. We build up much of this picture when we're young, learning from our parents, teachers, grandparents and our circumstances. Many of your beliefs might be based on what you heard at home while you were growing up. Perhaps you were told 'money doesn't grow on trees' or 'you need to eat everything on your plate'. You might even have seen your parents exhibit phobias. (Spider phobia anyone?) These beliefs can stay with us into adulthood and impact on how we live our lives without our even realising.

The thing to understand is that these beliefs are all stories we've made up to make sense of the world – and stories that can be altered at any point if we realise they no longer serve their purpose. These next tips, along with certain tools in the Self Care Toolkit, will help you challenge your own stories.

turning down critical fm

We all have an internal voice that speaks to us in what is more or less an ongoing dialogue, whether to warn us of danger, applaud us or criticise us if we feel we've done something badly. This voice has been called everything from the 'Chimp' to the 'Tiger' and the 'Saboteur', but my favourite name for it comes from Jess Baker, founder of Mimi Natural Skincare, who calls it 'Critical FM'.

First, let's look at where this voice comes from. Most likely its roots lie in our reptilian brain, the oldest part of the brain that is responsible for our habits, reflexes and the fight-or-flight reaction. This is the part of the brain that is responsible for keeping us safe and alive. In fact, its *only* purpose is to keep us safe and alive.

When you hear that internal voice criticising you, more than likely it's simply trying to stop you putting yourself at risk in some way. However, it's not always very helpful as it can prevent you from challenging yourself and moving forward. This part of the brain likes the status quo and it doesn't like change as change could mean danger; in fact, it's programmed to avoid change at all costs!

So, let's explore how to turn down Critical FM. Sit quietly for a few minutes and tune in to your inner voice. Listen intently to what it's saying. Now answer the following questions:

❊ What stories does your inner voice keep repeating? It might be things such as, 'I'm not good enough'; 'I'm stupid'; 'they'll find out at work I'm only pretending'; 'I'm not beautiful';

'I need to look different to be loved'; 'I need to earn more money to be happy'. What are your inner voice's favourite sayings?

❋ Where does this voice come from?

❋ Does it belong to someone you know?

❋ How does it make you feel?

Congratulations! You've met your inner critic, chimp, tiger, saboteur or whatever else you want to call it. Now you know who you're dealing with, you can start to question what it tells you, and turn down the volume when you need to.

managing your inner critic

You might well want to give your inner critic a name to make it easier to communicate with it. A client of mine realised she had an inner critic that focused purely on her earnings and money issues, and she called it 'Bert'. We often had sessions where we'd have a conversation with Bert. When I connected to my inner critic, I called her Anna. As well as naming your inner critic, perhaps give it a character or a silly voice to make it feel less serious and to help you identify the difference between 'it' and 'you'.

The key to managing this voice isn't by getting completely rid of it, because this is the same safety-conscious voice that will warn you it's not a good idea to jump off a cliff. (Kind of useful, right?) What you need to learn to do is *turn down the volume* of this voice when you want to, so you can make a decision that's right for you rather than one based on the scaremongering of your inner fears. To do this, try the following short exercise:

❋ What proof or evidence do you have that the stories your inner critic is telling you are true?

✳ In what ways might this proof or evidence be flawed or outdated?

✳ What other proof or evidence is there that contradicts the stories?

✳ When, specifically, has a story it's been telling you been wrong?

By building up a bank of evidence you will be able to challenge the stories – and thereby the beliefs – you've associated with yourself. Perhaps you were told as a child that you were clumsy, and have come to believe this about yourself, but when was the last time you actually tripped, fell or broke something? When we internalise beliefs and stories and never challenge them, they can hold us back.

The next time your inner critic shares its concerns for your welfare or flags up a warning, listen to it, thank it for sharing (you might even want to do this out loud), then decide how you want to move forward. This powerful technique means that you acknowledge the thought rather than keep trying to bat it away. When you thank your inner critic you're acknowledging there's a part of you that's trying to keep you safe; then you're able to make a decision based on your rational mind rather than from a place of fear.

put on your own oxygen mask first

When it comes to self care, there are many stories we tell ourselves, such as: 'it's selfish to put myself first'; 'to be a "good person" I need to care about other people'; 'my children are the most important thing in my world'; 'if I put myself first people won't like me'. The list is almost endless.

So, let me ask you, when was the last time you were on an aeroplane? Do you remember the safety instructions given by the flight crew, about fastening your seatbelt and on putting on life jackets? They tell you that if the air supply gets knocked out, your oxygen mask will come down from the ceiling. When they tell you how to put it on, they specifically instruct you to 'put on your own oxygen mask before helping others'.

The simple fact is you can't give from an empty well. If you're struggling to cope, if you can't breathe, how can you possibly help anyone else? Self care and looking after yourself actually enable you to be stronger for those that you love, to be able to help more effectively and to become a positive role model for the people around you.

banish 'all or nothing' thinking

Black and white thinking creates a problem as it only gives us two options. We're either brilliant or dreadful. Successful or worthless. Perfect or imperfect. *I can do that* or *I can't*. This way of thinking can create impossible standards for ourselves, leaving us little room for error. By limiting our choices and options, we set ourselves up for failure: we either have to be perfect in every way – or we're failures, which can lead to a lack of self-esteem, anxiety and many other issues. This kind of thinking can easily lead to us abandoning goals as we feel that if we make a 'mistake' then the whole thing is blown – and so we might as well not bother.

Give yourself permission to see the grey aspects of life. Allow yourself the possibility of growth and expansion. We're all on a journey and mistakes are how we grow and learn. Focus on the little wins and victories – on what you *can* do and what you *have* achieved.

One of the turning points for me on my recovery from bulimia was learning that another 'episode' didn't mean I'd failed. It didn't undo all the hard work and effort I'd put in; it simply meant I had a fresh opportunity to look at something I hadn't considered before and a new lesson to learn to help my recovery. It took me years to get to this point, but when I did it was one of the biggest turning points in my journey.

curiosity over judgment

You've met your inner critic and you've seen how 'all or nothing thinking' can limit your choices. The key to exploring these concepts is the idea of 'curiosity'. It's really easy for us to criticise ourselves and be our own worst critic, but that often leads us to judge and berate ourselves without seeking to understand *why* we may have behaved or experienced a particular situation. I encourage you to get curious with yourself. Instead of immediately jumping to judge or berate yourself, pause and explore *why it* happened and what you can learn from it.

set yourself up for inevitable success

Why do New Year's resolutions fail? Why do we abandon diets? Why, despite our best intentions, do we often not make it to the finish line of something we want to achieve? The simple answer is that we don't set ourselves up for success. That is, we try to achieve everything in leaps and bounds. If, for example, we take up a new exercise regime and promise to keep to it every day, but then miss a day or two, we might feel like we've failed, so we become unmotivated and our shiny new trainers collect dust.

It's far better to set smaller, easily attainable milestones for yourself so you stay committed and empowered. Think of it like running a marathon: you wouldn't turn up at the start line on the day of the race without having hit a series of milestones first during your training – and the same is true of any goal.

beautiful boundaries

Boundaries are a necessary and fundamental part of self care, relating to our physical, emotional, mental and spiritual wellbeing. They're the way we let the world know how to treat us, so try thinking of them as an invisible shield. Setting boundaries with your family, friends, colleagues and loved ones is vital and need not be as hard as you might think.

First, why don't we set boundaries? Often, it's because we want to please people and be liked. Yet by having no boundaries we effectively let everyone walk all over us. Boundaries enable us to protect our energy and our time. Your own boundaries will empower you to make decisions and take ownership of your actions, and signal to the world that you value yourself.

To help you define your personal boundaries ask yourself:

✳ What behaviours do I expect from others?

✳ What behaviours do I expect from myself?

✳ What does my body need to be truly nourished and to function well?

✳ What do I need to be at my best?

✳ What is my worst fear about saying no – and is it really likely to happen?

✳ What guilt do I need to let go of to live my life according to my own rules?

✳ When someone offends you, ask yourself these three things:

1. How much of this is about the other person?

2. How much of this is about me?

3. What do I need to do (if anything) to stand up for myself in this situation or to regain my personal power?

By answering these questions it should start to give you a picture of what you deem to be important and where your beautiful boundaries lie.

'Your primary job is to take care of yourself. You've got to decide to make your health and wellbeing your priority.'

Oprah Winfrey,
The Oprah Magazine

reprogramme your self-image

In Paul McKenna's book *Change Your Life in Seven Days*, he shares a powerful self-image reprogramming technique from Dr Maltz, based on the notion that our habits and imaginations play a more important part in shaping our behaviour than logic or willpower do.

Research has shown that the brain doesn't differentiate between 'real' experiences and 'imagined' experiences. This is why practices such as visualisations, setting positive intentions and guided meditations work so well, as they can be literally used to programme new neural pathways in the brain. The more you repeat this kind of work, the stronger the pathways become and the easier it is to automatically think new thoughts. Athletes and their coaches have exploited this fact for years, with many athletes visualising their performance before a race and

picturing themselves at their peak during it –
even before they step on the pitch, track or board.

The following guided meditation is closely
inspired by the work of Dr Maltz and is designed
to help you reprogramme your self-image.

* Switch off any electronic devices and sit or
  lie down somewhere where you won't be
  disturbed.
* Gently close your eyes and breathe deeply,
  allowing your body to relax and muscles to
  get heavier, and heavier.
* As you begin to relax even deeper, allow your
  mind and your imagination to wander.
* Allow thoughts and feelings to pass by and
  just let them go without holding onto any
  of them.
* Now visualise another being standing in
  front of you. This individual represents the
  best possible version of yourself that you
  can imagine.

✳ Take a moment to truly witness this individual and feel its presence.

✳ What does this person look like? How does he or she sound? What sort of energy surrounds them? In what ways might this person speak to others? How do they navigate life? What makes them strong? How do they manage life or handle problems and set goals? How does this person make you feel?

✳ What else do you notice about this version of you? Absorb everything from this interaction.

✳ Take a moment to become totally at ease with this version of your best self. Allow yourself to acknowledge all the positive aspects of the best version of you.

✳ Now, step into your best self as if you're pulling on a coat, zipping up a onesie or slipping on a dress. Look through that self's eyes, feel through that self's fingers and hear through that self's ears. Feels good, doesn't it?

✻ Now you have fully merged into this best self, visualise the various ways in which your life might be different living from this vantage point. What situations would be different? What relationships? What new or different ways would you experience the world?

✻ When you have taken all the information you need, gently open your eyes and come back to the room and spend a few minutes capturing your thoughts and feelings after this exercise.

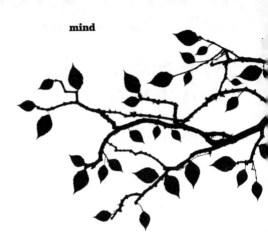

'One comes to believe whatever one repeats to oneself sufficiently often, whether the statement be true or false.'

Robert Collier,
The Secret of Power

the power of positive affirmations

Positive affirmations build new neural pathways in our brains through the repetition of sentences or phrases. It's a bit like building up strength through weightlifting: the more you repeat a phrase, the stronger your brain's link with it becomes, and the more quickly and easily your brain is able to access a particular thought.

Here's how to create a positive affirmation:

❋ Put the affirmation in the first person; for example: 'I can make a valuable contribution to the lives of other people.'

❋ Keep it in the present tense; for example: 'I am in charge of my destiny' or 'I have many gifts to offer the world.'

❋ Make it *really* positive.

❋ Make it realistic; for example, if you're a really nervous speaker, saying 'I am the best public speaker' might not strike you as being believable, whereas 'I am a good public speaker' or 'I am a capable public speaker' would be more believable.

✳ Create one or two affirmations of your own and repeat them often, perhaps fifteen times in the morning and fifteen times in the evening.

overcoming perfectionism

The pressure to be perfect and 'always on' can be overwhelming. Whether the aim is to be the perfect boss, employee, partner, sibling or to have the perfect life, home, children, body, there is a never-ending stream of 'perfectionism' which our generation is struggling to keep up with.

Whilst the traits of perfectionists are often applauded and even encouraged, psychologists have found there is a tipping point at which perfectionism can backfire and become an impediment. Perfectionism has been shown to have serious implications for our health, increasing our risk of burn-out, mental health disorders, stress and anxiety. As a result, it also lowers the immune system, making us more likely to pick up bugs and illnesses.

Rather than strive for perfection, strive for progress, for growth and for the opportunity to learn. Imperfect action is always better than perfect inaction. Keep a record of what you've achieved and how far you've come as a way to remind yourself how much you've progressed. You might like to have a special notebook or beautiful diary that you use for this purpose.

'You were born to
be real, not perfect.'

**Ralph Marston,
The Daily Motivator**

comparison is the thief of joy

Psychologists believe that we all have the hardwired tendency to assess our self-worth by comparing ourselves to other people. However, with the rise of social media and the internet we're no longer just comparing ourselves to our friends and co-workers. We're now looking at celebrities 24/7 and have access to people we never did before. Suddenly it's possible to compare our lives to almost everyone else on the planet.

For some of us, using social media and browsing the internet can be a useful, positive and connected experience. However, there can be less favourable outcomes for many of us when we can start to see social media impact on our mental wellbeing, feelings of self-esteem and general levels of happiness. If that's the case, it might be time to do a digital audit.

✳ Notice which websites make you feel bad. Experiment with not visiting them or limiting the amount you visit them for the next week, and see how that affects your mood.

✳ Unfollow/block anyone on social media who drags you down or causes you to start comparing your life negatively against theirs.

✳ Choose one day a week where you switch off completely and live in the real world for the full twenty-four hours.

✳ Limit your internet usage in the evenings (especially the hour before you go to bed).

'Don't compare your worst bits to someone else's highlight reel.'

practise gratitude

When we regularly take time out to notice all the good things in our lives, we can quickly turn around negativity, anxiousness or comparativeness. There are numerous studies and pieces of research that show gratitude positively impacts our mental wellbeing and encourages us to seek out more positivity in our lives.

To develop a gratitude practice:

* Keep a gratitude jar. At the end of each day, make a note of something you're grateful for and pop it in the jar. As a bonus, empty the jar on New Year's Eve and look back over the whole year.
* Every morning or night, state three things you're grateful for.
* Keep a gratitude diary and capture in it at least one thing every day you're grateful for

– which will in turn inspire you to look for more things to be grateful for.

✳ Notice at least one thing every day you're grateful for and share it with a 'gratitude buddy'.

Aim to be as specific as possible and find something new to be grateful for each day – it could be gratitude for the sunrise in the morning, or for someone giving you a warm drink on a cold day. Look for the small pleasures as well as the bigger, more obvious things.

obsess about what you love!

Another fascinating fact about the brain is that, when we focus on something, we start drawing all of our attention to it. So, if you develop an interest in red cars, for instance, suddenly you'll start seeing them everywhere! Similarly, if you're drawn to bad news, you're likely to hear it wherever you go. Our brains make us aware of every possible instance in which a piece of information might help in the current situation, such as past memories and experiences, as well as new information to help us understand the current situation better and make decisions about it.

Far better then, to focus on what you love about your life, about yourself, about your work, your family and friends. Rather than obsess and worry about things, or focus on the negatives, feed yourself with positivity wherever you can.

the compliment challenge

For the next seven days, every time someone compliments you, simply smile and say thank you. Don't push the compliment aside, dismiss it or downplay it, or jump in to return it; just acknowledge it and accept it for the gift it is. As uncomfortable as it may feel at first, you'll soon start to find it easier to accept compliments and to appreciate feedback from the people around you.

At the same time over the next seven days, compliment other people when you see them do something well or when you notice something else you feel deserves attention. How does it feel when they light up and accept the compliment compared to when someone downplays a compliment or rejects it?

managing stress and anxiety

We all tend to worry and get anxious about things. But what happens when our worries and stress tip over into something more serious?

Our brain is wired to cope with stress in the same way it's done for millennia: it fights it, runs from it or freezes in the face of it. As amazing as our brains are, we haven't yet evolved enough to distinguish between a stressful job interview and running from a predator.

When our body goes into flight or fight mode, the brain does some pretty incredible things. First, it floods the body with cortisol and adrenaline to prepare it for fight or flight. Then it redirects blood away from the organs to our limbs so we're prepared for the right response. Our impulses quicken, our attention sharpens and we prepare to fight the 'enemy'. Only the enemy isn't a sabre-toothed tiger or a dinosaur or a rival tribe looking to plunder our village. It's much more likely to be our boss, the rush hour, our partner, or someone we probably can't run from and really shouldn't attack.

There is overwhelming evidence that, if we don't manage our stress over time, our bodies and overall wellbeing can be impacted, resulting in symptoms such as headaches and IBS, disorders of the immune system and hormonal imbalances, and conditions such as chronic fatigue syndrome and depression.

Typically, our stress is focused on what happened in the past or what should be happening in the future. What causes the problem for us is our perception of how things *should be* instead.

So how do we move our thoughts from a state of stress and anxiety to one of calm and relaxation? Here are some simple yet effective practices:

❋ Keep a thought log (check out the Self Care Toolkit on page 199 for an example).

❋ Write your own 'morning pages'. In her brilliant book *The Artist's Way*, Julia Cameron explains the benefits of writing from a stream of consciousness each

morning until you've covered two pages.
Many people who follow this practice report
having a clearer head and a calmer outlook.

* Practise the three to five breathing
technique. In yoga, a simple *pranayama* (or
breathing technique) at the start of many
exercises involves breathing in for a count
of three and out for a count of five. This
slow and steady way of breathing sends a
message to the nervous system that it's safe
to relax.

* Take a walk in nature.

* Call a trusted and honest friend, and talk
through your worries.

* Ask yourself 'What problem do I have at
this precise moment?' Not in the future, but
right now? Often you'll realise your stress is
based on a perception of what 'might' be.

* Work with a coach or therapist if you feel
that stress and anxiety are affecting your
daily life.

mindfulness

It's easy to stop noticing the world around us.
When we're busy rushing to work, juggling
commitments and dealing with the stresses of
modern life, we can often live in our heads and
lose connection with our bodies and the world
around us. Mindfulness is about practising being
in the present moment. It means noticing the
sounds, smells, sights, feelings and emotions
we are having and allowing ourselves the time
to process these things. Mindfulness positively
impacts on wellbeing and can be applied to almost
any situation. It is a really powerful tool for
managing food and cravings, stress and anxiety.

✳ Try something new such as sitting in a
different carriage on the train, getting up a
few minutes earlier than normal, taking a
different route to work or going somewhere
new for lunch. Focus your attention. How

does it compare to your usual routine?
Making a small change can be a great way to
see the world afresh.

* Slow down and notice what you're feeling
  and thinking. Interrupt your internal
  autopilot by naming your thoughts and
  feelings, which you might find easier to
  do when you're in motion, such as when
  walking or practising yoga or tai chi.

* When you eat, take the time to notice the
  smell of your food, its colours and textures
  before you put anything in your mouth.
  When you take each bite move the mouthful
  slowly around your mouth and notice its
  flavours, temperature and any sensations
  you feel. Mindful eating will help you
  connect with your hunger and pay more
  attention to your fullness cues, making
  you feel more satisfied – plus, you'll likely
  discover a lot about the food you eat!

* Take a mindfulness course.

meditation

Meditation has been practised for centuries
for good reason. It reduces stress, improves
concentration, benefits the immune system,
increases happiness and emotional wellbeing,
and improves mental health and self-esteem.
Think of meditation as the ultimate 'me time'
– an instant chill pill. It's an opportunity to
reset and recharge your brain in much the same
way you would charge your phone or laptop.
Meditation means intentionally setting aside
time to do something good for yourself.

'You should sit in
meditation for
twenty minutes every
day – unless you're too
busy; then you should
sit for an hour.'
Zen Proverb

When are good times to meditate?

❋ First thing in the morning when you
   wake up.
❋ On your morning commute.
❋ During your lunchbreak.
❋ On the commute on the way home.
❋ Before you go to bed.
❋ When you exercise, or go for a walk.

From transcendental meditation in which
you repeat mantras, to mindful meditation in
which you focus on your breathing, to guided
meditations or moving meditation – there really
is a meditation practice to suit everyone. Try
some different types to discover what works
best for you. You might notice your mind goes
somewhere else when you exercise. Or perhaps
your thoughts switch off when you listen to
stories or the radio. How about when you take
a yoga class or breathe deeply? Look for clues

about the way your mind naturally softens and relaxes, as this will give you an idea about which type of meditation to try first.

Here are some ideas to get you started:

✳ Download an app such as Headspace and listen to it during your daily commute.

✳ Join a free online meditation course like those offered by Deepak Chopra and Oprah Winfrey.

✳ Practise closing your eyes and breathing in for five and out for five, letting your thoughts drift by like clouds.

✳ Start small by meditating for just a minute or two a day to begin with.

✳ Download a guided visualisation.

✳ Go for a walk in nature and simply look at the trees, the grass, the animals and the world around you. Allow your mind to focus only on these things.

decide to be happy

When you ask people what they want from life the answer is often simple: 'to be happy'. Yet so many of us look for happiness in the wrong place. We might believe happiness will come when we've lost weight, got a promotion, earned a certain amount of money or found the love of our lives. We delay experiencing our current happiness as if it's somehow not valid, or as if it's something that needs to be bestowed on us from outside.

Happiness can be found here and now. Lynn Hord, The Joy Coach, says that moments of happiness abound in everyday life and can come from little things: a delicious flat white in a buzzy café, a hug, watching a bird flit about the garden, laughing with a friend, cuddling the dog, revelling in satisfying work, appreciating the sunshine or spending time with a friend.

When you start to pay attention to these moments of joy, the gaps in between become smaller, and the amount of time you feel happy increases. So you really don't have to delay experiencing happiness; you can choose, right now, to start focusing on the things in your life that make you feel good, and through that focus you will start to feel happier more of the time.

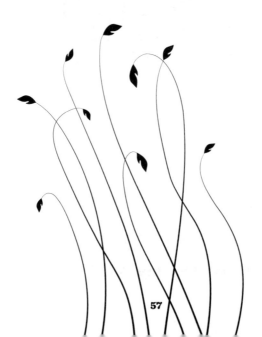

'Happiness isn't a
switch that's on or off,
it's something you grow.'
Lynn Hord, The Joy Coach

boost your happiness

Here are some simple things you can do right now to increase your happiness:

❋ Write a list of twenty things in your life that are great right now, and which make you happy – and keep adding to it.

❋ Choose a happy song to play to lift your mood whenever you need it.

❋ Select a 'happy' song to use as your daily alarm clock (beats that loud buzzer).

❋ List ten activities you can do that don't require any money that make you happy. (Having a picnic in the park is one of my personal favourites!)

❋ Create or buy a happiness planner and plan for your happiness. What small actions can you take each day, week or month that make you happy?

✳ Consider simplifying your life in some way. What things truly add value and meaning to your life and what things might be more temporary distractions?

✳ Before you speak, act, buy a book or new piece of clothing, ask yourself if it sparks joy and will increase your happiness.

✳ Create a morning ritual to start your day with a smile – it might be meditating, morning pages, an exercise class, taking a walk – whatever it is for you that makes you smile.

the illusion of busyness

I bet you've uttered the words 'sorry, I'm busy!' at some point during the last week. Heck, I'd guess at some point in the last twelve hours! Our lives are a seemingly never-ending to-do list. Work pressures, paying bills, managing a home, a

social life, emotional issues, keeping on top of the
latest must-see TV series. It's no wonder I often
hear people tell me 'there aren't enough hours
in the day'. But here's the thing, we all have the
same twenty-four hours a day; it's the one magic
leveller, whether we are Richard Branson, Oprah,
the Queen, Beyoncé, Jane down the road or Ben
in finance.

So, what's the difference?

It's in how we *use* the time.

Recent surveys have shown that working
overtime is firmly embedded in the UK's working
culture, with an incredible three-quarters of us
routinely working late in the office or at home.
Many of us also work through our lunchbreaks
or at the weekends. Right now, as you sit here
reading this, there's an army of busy people
furiously charging through their to-do lists,
crossing off meetings, days, weeks and years
of their lives. I have met so many people who
believe sacrificing life now will ensure a better

future. Allow me to let you in on a secret: exhausting yourself now only means you're missing out on your current happiness.

The truth is that 'busyness' doesn't lead to a happier, healthier or more successful life. If anything, it prevents you from truly living. Busyness becomes an excuse that can be used to mask fear and insecurities – and a hiding place. Here are six tips to help you jump off the busyness treadmill:

1. Define your version of success

In the workplace, a job title, pay grade, corner office or doing great work that you're proud of could all be ways to measure success. In life, we can measure success by our earnings or possessions, time spent with loved ones or special experiences, or any number of things.

The question you need to ask yourself is what success means to you. What do you *really* want, and what are you being told by others that you *should* be aiming for? There are no right or wrong answers; it's just important to be clear about what your definition of success means, so you can more easily attain it and live according to your own values and priorities.

2. *Be ruthless about how and where you spend your time*

When you lie on your deathbed I'm certain you'll want to look back at a full and happy life, surrounded by loved ones, with memories of the time you spent together. Time is the one commodity we spend and never get back. As a busy person myself, one of the best pieces of advice I was ever given was to apply the two-question rule:

* Am I truly adding value by being here?
* Is this the very best use of my time?

If the answer is 'no' to either question – step back and re-evaluate.

Another great exercise to help understand where and how we're spending our time is called 'Yes to This, No to That'. Saying yes to spending your time in one way means saying no to something else. For example, saying yes to a last minute catch-up with a friend might mean saying no to an early night. Or saying yes to an extra piece of work could mean missing a different deadline. There's usually not a right or wrong answer, but this exercise will enable you, very quickly, to understand that your time is finite, and gives you the chance to evaluate a decision *before* automatically saying yes! (You'll find a table you can use for this exercise in the Self Care Toolkit on page 201.)

3. Review how you spend your time

Use your diary as a way to keep your priorities in check. At the start of each month outline what your priorities are. You might, for instance, write down 'family', 'work', 'exercise', 'health', 'finances'. Give each priority a colour code in your diary. Note every appointment and how you spend your time in the appropriate colour. At the end of each week look back over your diary to see how you've spent your days. What areas might need to be reprioritised, or which took up too much of your time unnecessarily? This is a quick and easy way to see at a glance how your time has been spent. If you like, instead of using colour coding, simply review your diary at the end of the week and give yourself a score out of five or ten per key area.

4. Know your 'non-negotiables'

Have you ever said yes to an evening out or work situation when you knew that doing so would mean you don't get the time to do something for yourself? In my twenties, I was known for doing more in a morning than some friends did in a week, cramming in exercise, work and socialising. After my body sent me very clear signals that enough was enough, I realised I needed to prioritise some downtime. I set about blocking time in my diary that became 'me time' and appointments with myself to rest, exercise and take better care of myself. These 'me time' appointments have become my non-negotiables, set in stone.

What would be your non-negotiables with your time? Is it a gym class you love each week? A course you're taking? Date night with your partner? What has to change for you to keep that time sacred each week? Make a sacred, non-negotiable appointment with yourself and honour it!

5. Be respectful of your time as well as other people's time

Time is a precious commodity for all of us and giving our time is one of the biggest gifts we can bestow. Likewise, if someone gives you their time, it's a privilege. Consider how you treat not just your time but that of others – do you arrive at meetings and appointments punctually or are you always late? Do you simply forward emails or do you provide a summary, or outline why you've sent it? Do you prepare for meetings and events, or turn up and wing it? Are you someone who sends late requests for things, or who plans ahead?

How we treat others is so often a reflection of how we treat ourselves. It's not about being perfect as sometimes life gets in the way and unexpected things happen. (Welcome to the real world!) However, if you notice a consistent disruptive pattern in your attitude to time – both your own and other people's – now is the moment to revisit the way you manage it.

6. Create space

Hands up if you like to feel productive. Me too. We all want to feel needed, useful, purposeful and valued. For many of us, we measure this by how much we *do*. We fill our diaries with hundreds of engagements and appointments. We write to-do lists. (Oh my God, the piles of 'to-do' lists!) We commit to causes, join clubs and attend parent associations meetings. So many of us find it hard to simply relax and just *be*. Often, it's not 'balance' we seek but 'space'. Space to think, to breathe, to relax and reconnect. This is why meditating and spending time in nature are so valuable to our mental wellbeing, because these create space for us, allowing our minds to enjoy a quiet moment.

Create space in your diary after meetings to absorb the learnings or to consider the next steps. When you take a course or class, leave space around the start and end of it in which to truly embed and absorb the lessons. Create space in your diary too for downtime and relaxation: think of it as an appointment with yourself – no cleaning, chores, catching up on social media or emails – just relax.

'You make the decisions on what you will allow into your life and to mask everything by not expecting of others what they expect of you is not being honest about your own self care and what you want from your own life.'

**Angela Harkness,
Life and Business Coach**

be your own guru

It's easy to hand over power to other people. By handing the responsibility of decision-making to people and authorities other than ourselves, we effectively relinquish responsibility for the outcome. We look for external sources to validate the decisions we make, the paths we take, the self-development we undertake.

Yet you don't need gold stars, certificates, gold standards or external validation to be successful in life. You *are* the wisdom of you.

Yes, you can seek guidance or support if needed. Yes, learning new things can empower and enrich you. Yes, new skills and hobbies will embolden you. But YOU are the best authority on you.

self care takeaway tips

※ Self care starts in your mind – learn to turn down the volume on Critical FM.

※ Focus on the good stuff with affirmations and by practising gratitude.

※ Set yourself realistic goals – and take small steps to achieve them.

※ Prioritise your self care, and treat your time like the precious commodity it is.

※ *Do* less and *be* more: discover the benefits of taking time out, and of practices such as mindfulness and meditation.

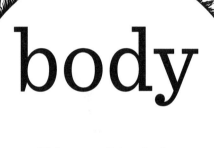

body

'Take care of your body,
it's the only place you have to live.'
Jim Rhon

Pounding the treadmill. Sweating through spin class. Juicing. Detoxing. Dieting. Being 'good'. Being 'bad'. Cleansing. Bingeing. Trying to tame the beast and beat it into submission. Using holidays as 'thinspiration' to kick start a new diet. Eating to numb feelings. 'No carbs before Marbs' style programmes...

When you've quite literally been at war with your body for years, when the fight is all you know, how do you turn it around? It's little wonder the most common question I get asked is: 'Is it really possible to love your body?'

I'm happy to tell you the answer is yes.

But first, how have we got here?

It's fair to say we have complicated relationships with our bodies , with millions of us suffering from all types of eating disorders and disordered eating patterns. Whilst 'body issues' are often seen to be a female matter, make no mistake – men and women struggle equally with body image. We all have feelings and thoughts about the way we look. And we've all got particular ideas and feelings about the ways in which other people perceive us.

These opinions, thoughts and feelings about our bodies come from a myriad of places. As we've already seen, we form opinions at a very young age about the world, taking our cues from people we trust such as our parents, friends and teachers, as well as from society. Certainly, in the West, bodies have been objectified for decades, with everything from Disney movies to magazines telling us how we should look – although that 'look' may have changed dramatically over the years.

When it comes to physical self care, it's little surprise, then, that we can often fall into the

trap of assuming it's just about what we eat or
how hard we exercise, and that we have to look a
certain way to be healthy, happy or attractive. But
healthy, happy bodies come in many shapes and
sizes, and physical self care means nourishing
our bodies through many different aspects: sleep,
food, regular physical movement, sunshine,
positive thoughts and much more. And I use the
word 'nourishing' purposefully. For many of us,
our physical bodies have become a battle ground,
a place to punish ourselves, which is why my
intention in this part of the book is to show you
how to fall in love with your body and give it the
care that it – and you – deserve.

However, this part of the book isn't going
to include recipes or tell you what to eat or
how many burpees to do. When it comes to
regulating our eating habits, we don't need
to go to extremes or follow fads. Deep down,
we all instinctively know what to eat. (If you
want specific dietary advice you can visit a

nutritionist or find thousands of articles, books and blogs on the subject). If you want exercise advice you can turn to any number of sources or personal trainers. Instead, in this section, my intention is to give you simple, effective and useful self care tips that can make a difference to how you eat, how you exercise and how you treat your body. From this place, I hope you'll be able to make better life choices.

stop judging yourself on a number

Your weight. Your dress size. Your BMI. Your calorie intake. Your waist circumference. When did all these numbers start to have such an impact? It's amazing how we allow these things to determine how we feel each day. But what if you decided here and now to focus on how you feel, rather than on numbers like those?

One of the best things you can do is to get rid of the scales. Yes, you read that right, just get rid of them! The only times you really need to know what you weigh is when you're pregnant or if you're on a specific healthcare or training programme, and, to be honest, you don't even need to know then – your doctor or practitioner does, and they'll have their own set of scales (promise!). So go ahead and dump the scales. If you're not quite ready to throw them out, try putting them out of sight in a cupboard or wardrobe to reduce your dependence on them.

When it comes to clothes, sizes can vary from store to store. At best, clothes sizes are just a guide. Far better to wear something that fits you properly and makes you feel good than to try to squeeze into clothes that are too small for you or which hide your body away in the equivalent of a bin liner.

'Choose your clothes because of how they fit you and make you feel rather than because of what it says on the label.'

**Susie Hasler,
Styled by Susie**

focus on your good bits

How many times have you stood in front of the mirror and critiqued your body? I bet it runs into the thousands. Many of us may have even stopped looking in the mirror because we don't like what we see. Yet our bodies are incredible works of nature: they come in all different shapes and sizes, and every one of them is miraculous.

If you simply stop and consider the odds against any one of us being born, it's actually remarkable that any of us are here at all. So, next time you look in the mirror, instead of focusing on your wobbly bits and the bits you don't like or feel embarrassed about, focus on what you *do* like. Even if that's your toes or a little finger. Look at one part of your body you like and send it love; focus on how much you like that part – and focus only on that. Do this every time you look in the mirror. Then, each week add another part of your body to your 'love' list.

remember, beauty is more than just your body

Your mind, your sense of humour, your intelligence, the skills you have, the way you make people feel – there are so many facets of beauty beyond your physical form. Beauty is a state of mind, not a body state.

As an easy way to remember this, buy a beautiful little notebook and write a list of things you like about yourself and any achievements that you're proud of. I challenge you to start your list with fifty things and to keep on adding to it. You could ask your trusted loved ones to share what they believe makes you beautiful, which will often lead to some powerful revelations and new perspectives.

Another way to support yourself is to stop consuming any media that makes you feel anything other than great. Besides doing a digital audit (see page 40), stop buying magazines if they make you feel rubbish after reading them. And if certain friends don't say nice things about you, maybe reduce the amount of time you spend with them and spend time instead with people who make you feel good.

learn about your body shape

Clothes and the way we dress ourselves can really impact on the way we feel about ourselves. From wearing the right underwear to picking clothes that show off your best bits, learning about your body shape and how to dress yourself to make the most of it can have a real impact on your self-esteem and the way you perceive yourself physically. The way we dress and present ourselves are also the first pieces of information we give to the world about ourselves. So what do they say about you?

If you really don't know what suits you or what works for your shape, do a little research. Perhaps pay for a session with a professional stylist, or use one of the free styling services provided by many major high-street stores, which will help you appreciate your body as it is. It will also inspire you to try new things and work with your shape in a new way.

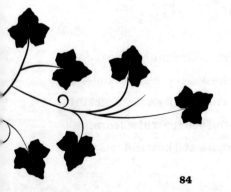

write a love letter to your body

Our bodies are remarkable. We're constantly renewing ourselves at a cellular level; our heart beats without us thinking about it; and our immune system fights illnesses and threats without us even realising. And that's not even scratching the surface of all the remarkable things our bodies do for us.

When you consider just how remarkable your body is – the experiences it's allowed you to have and the way it enables you to live your life – it soon becomes pretty obvious that judging it merely because it doesn't fit the supermodel mould might not exactly be fair.

So carve out an hour to sit down and write your body a love letter. Don't underestimate the power of this – DO IT! Give yourself permission to be honest and open, and just write what comes.

Include the things that you're grateful for; forgive it if you need to; and acknowledge all the things it does for you.

If you like, instead of writing to it, you could draw a picture, make a mood board or pen a song. Get creative – it's your love letter!

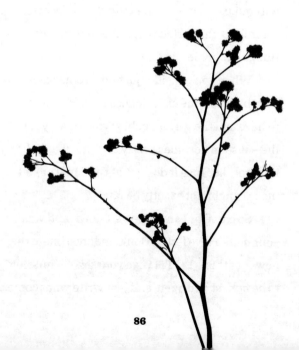

'Body confidence doesn't come from having the perfect body, it comes from accepting the one you've already got.'
Oprah Winfrey

emotional hunger vs true hunger?

When it comes to food and how we feel about our bodies, we often try to cure the symptom rather than dealing with the underlying issues. Commonly we do this through dieting, in the misguided belief that we need to be a certain size for our life to transform. Have you ever thought, 'If I can just be X pounds lighter/heavier, I'll be happier?' I know I have.

It's far easier to blame our unhappiness on something that we can try to manage and control, rather than admit our unhappiness might have a deeper emotional cause. It's time to get to know the difference between true hunger and emotional hunger.

We eat to satisfy and maintain the needs of the body. This is the reason for true hunger. But of course, we're also emotional beings, and we

eat to satisfy the needs of our minds, out of habit
and from triggers in the world around us as well.
These triggers could be environmental factors
– like having an ice cream when the sun comes
out or eating chestnuts at Christmas. We also
eat and drink from emotional triggers, such as
eating chocolate as a pick-me-up treat or sipping
a glass of wine to unwind at the end of a stressful
day. There are many different reasons *why* we
eat and, in the Self Care Toolkit on pages 203
to 205, you'll find a table listing the differences
between physical and emotional hunger, and a
handy food log to help you start to identify your
own eating habits.

Notice what triggers certain eating habits
of yours; what patterns are there? Getting to
understand our personal habits is the first step
to establishing a healthy relationship with food.
When you know *why* you eat, you'll be well on
the way to making better informed food choices
for yourself.

ban the diet!

The word 'diet' comes from the Latin *diaeta*, which means 'to live life'. Only we've taken it to mean something completely different. The way you eat is actually part of your ongoing lifestyle, not a race to get the perfect beach body, or fit into a wedding gown or that little black dress at Christmas. One cake or cookie isn't going to make any more of a difference than one salad or smoothie to your health or to your figure; it's the overall way you live your life and nourish your body that counts.

Our bodies are all different and just because one style of eating works for one person, it doesn't necessarily mean it will work for another. In addition, eating well is not about extremes, but about learning how to eat a varied and balanced diet that gives you the nutrients, minerals and fuel that are vital for your body and brain to function properly. And that is different for all of us.

Besides banning the word 'diet', we also need to ban words like 'sin', 'naughty', 'dirty' and 'cheat' from our food vocabulary. No food is inherently evil, unless of course it's rancid or starting to grow fungus. However, there are foods that have higher nutritional values and give us greater energy such as fruit, vegetables, grains, and meat compared to those that are more indulgent, such as chocolate and cake. Get into the habit of noticing and increasing the foods that give you energy and enjoying the more indulgent foods less frequently. When you start to eat more of the high energy, healthy foods you naturally crowd out the more indulgent food.

focus on food you *can* have, rather than food you *can't*

As you've seen, we need to ban a diet mentality from our world. A diet mentality restricts foods, creates a list of 'banned' foods and sets up a situation where we're more focused on what we can't have than what we can. This is made worse by the fact our brains don't process negatives, which means that if we're saying to ourselves 'don't have the biscuits, don't have the biscuits', all we actually hear is 'have the biscuits, have the biscuits'! Instead, focus on all the wonderful food you *can* eat and enjoy new tastes and flavours.

eat good, feel good

To get the most out of your meals, focus on eating real food (i.e. food that isn't processed) and choose food to eat that is as close to the natural source as possible. You know what real food is: stuff that doesn't come in a packet with an ingredients list longer than the cast of *Game of Thrones*.

When it comes to calorie counting, yes, on a simplistic scale calories in and calories out is how to manage weight loss. But not all calories are equal: if you ate 1,000 calories of broccoli and 1,000 calories of ice cream, you'd notice the difference. Instead of counting calories, count ingredients. Choose foods with as few ingredients in the list as possible (i.e. real food!).

If you're feeling a bit 'meh' you'll have a far better chance of feeling better if you fuel your body with nutritious food to help it fire on all cylinders.

make healthy eating convenient

We are creatures of habit and convenience. And we will almost always choose the path of least resistance.

Making healthy eating convenient is simply about making the healthy choice easier to select. It's been shown that people who have a bowl of fruit readily available on their desk or kitchen worktop will automatically eat more of it; whereas those with bowls of chocolate on their desk – yes, you guessed it – will eat more chocolate.

A simple way to make healthy food convenient is to keep it at eye level and within arm's reach. Store healthy food in your fridge, larder and cupboards where it'll be the first thing you see. Have healthy snacks like fruit and nuts available at work and in your bag so if you're hungry you reach for these, rather than less healthy options that will simply spike your blood sugar for a short while before bringing you crashing down.

It's all about being prepared. If you get hungry while you're on the go, you might be tempted to nip into the nearest shop and buy whatever is to hand, unless you have healthy options with you. Likewise, if you come home from work and can't be bothered to cook or prepare anything, storing provisions of pre-prepared food or food frozen from a previous batch can make all the difference between having a healthy meal or not (see page 101).

make healthy food attractive and appetising

Let's face it, we eat with our eyes as well as our stomachs. So, use nice crockery, make your meals colourful, and, if you're preparing food, think about how best to serve it. You don't need to be a Michelin-starred chef to make your food look good! Making food that's as attractive to the eye as it is to the taste buds will increase your desire to eat it in the first place, and improve your levels of satisfaction afterwards. This approach is especially powerful with children!

If we're just cooking for one, it's can be easy to become a bit lazy or think it's too much hassle to cook for ourselves. But let's look at this in a different way – after all, who is more deserving of a beautiful, nourishing meal than you are? Even if you eat alone, take the time to make your meal look appetising, set a place for yourself at the table and treat yourself with the same love and care as you would if you were entertaining a guest.

create a new normal

We all want to eat in a way that we believe is 'normal'. And the habits and language we develop around food are a clear way to signal to ourselves what 'normal' eating is. If you eat takeaways every weekend, this becomes a 'normal' habit. Whereas if you associate fruit and vegetables with 'dieting' or 'restriction', then eating them won't be your 'normal' but rather some kind of punishing regime.

What could a new normal be for you? Perhaps adding a bowl of salad to your dinner table? Or making a fruit salad every morning to take to work? Or adding fresh vegetables to every meal? There are many ways to normalise healthy eating – whatever you do, make it fun!

'Being healthy has become so confusing and convoluted these days. People think they need to be taking things to the extreme. But improving your health can be achieved by shifting habits to include more real food in your diet while still being a regular member of society.'

**Chris Sandel,
Nutritionist, 7 Health**

slow down...

So much of what we do now, we do fast. We grab breakfast on the go. Eat lunch at our desk. Rustle up dinner in a flash. We order things online and they're with us in an hour. We hurry to and from our meetings. We're all so busy rushing from place to place that we don't take time out to eat properly. This can mean we don't really taste our food and eat too quickly for our bodies to feel satisfied, with the result that we end up eating more than we should or craving food later to fill a perceived gap.

To eat well:

✳ Aim to make your meal last for twenty minutes (at least). Start playing a game with yourself and increase the time you take to eat each meal. If you take three minutes now, aim to make it five at the next meal and then increase it slowly, ideally until your meals are twenty minutes.

❋ Put your knife and fork down between bites.

❋ Eat at a table away from the TV, your phone
or your desk, and focus only on eating.

❋ Don't multitask!

❋ Eat mindfully, noticing every mouthful:
what's the colour, smell and look of the food?
What's the temperature, texture, taste and
sensation when you put it in your mouth?

cook up some fun

Cooking every day can quickly become a chore,
especially if you've had a big day at work and
come home to face the fridge. So you might find
that injecting some fun back into making meals
is a sure-fire way to reignite your interest, as well
as a chance to learn new skills.

I love using my travels to inspire my
cooking. Picking a country on the map and then
researching recipes from that place can be a

great way to fuel a travel addiction as well as inspire meals.

Other ways include swapping recipes or cookbooks with friends, or picking a new ingredient and finding recipes based on that ingredient. See what works for you.

batch cook

If there's one single, simple way to improve how you eat, it would be through batch cooking. Making large stews, chillies, dahl or salads, and prepping vegetables, means you cook once and can then store healthy, homemade, gorgeous food ready for those too-busy days, tired days and the I-can't-be-bothered-to-cook kind of days. All you need is a good stock of Tupperware, a spare evening and a good recipe or two.

shop online

This is a game changer. Not only does shopping online for food save time and money, it also means you only buy food that you really want to have in the house. It's far easier to avoid indulgent or unhealthy foods if they're not in the cupboards, and it's even easier to stop yourself buying them when you shop online.

A top tip is to set up a favourites list so you can make your shop even simpler and quicker.

clear your kitchen clutter

Go through your fridge, larder, cupboards and drawers and discard *any* food or jars that are past their use-by date, or which have been opened and not consumed within the recommended time. Also dispose of any foods you are tempted to binge on, or which you reward yourself with even though you know it isn't what you really want to be eating, or which make you feel guilty or bad once you have eaten them. If you don't have this stuff in the house you're more likely to make more positive food choices for yourself.

When you've done this, clear out any old broken crockery. Eating off chipped, stained and worn crockery just doesn't make food look visually appealing. Donate your old stuff to charity if you like, and replace it with new kitchenware. You don't have to spend a lot of money; lots of stores sell attractive crockery that you can buy without breaking the bank.

easy food swaps

We make around 200 food choices a day, many of which don't even enter our consciousness because we make them automatically. It's far easier to create a new habit by mirroring an old habit, even an unconscious one. For example, if you know you tend to eat sweets at 4 p.m. because your energy levels are low, swap the sweets for fruit or nuts instead. If you always have a cup of coffee on the way to work, switch the coffee for water so you can increase your water consumption.

Equally, if you're trying to make bigger changes to your diet, like increasing your meat-free days, start small and make easy changes. Maybe make one meal a week meat free and build this up to a whole day. It's better to make small, easy changes that you can stick to than go for all or nothing, as when you succeed in small ways, you will be rewarded with a sense of achievement, have a chance to see the benefits and be motivated to keep with it!

start the day with water and lemon

If there was one thing I wish I could get every person I know to do, it's to start their day with lemon and water. It's one of the quickest, easiest and simplest health hacks out there and it takes two seconds (literally!).

Before you eat or drink anything else in the morning, pour yourself a glass of water (ideally, water that's at room temperature) and add a slice of lemon to the glass.

The benefits include better digestion and increased hydration; plus a glass of lemon and water will start your day with a healthy dose of vitamin C and a potassium boost.

After drinking the water, wait about twenty minutes before brushing your teeth (if you haven't already brushed them) as the acid from the lemon can soften the enamel, making it more prone to erosion during brushing.

add a glass of water to your day

Dehydration can creep up on us, especially if we work in air-conditioned buildings. If you're feeling sluggish, distracted and, well, a bit lacklustre, add a glass of water to your day or swap your mid-morning coffee with a glass of water instead. In my online resources, I share a 'how to' water guide to inspire you to increase your water intake on a daily basis (visit: melnoakes.com/book).

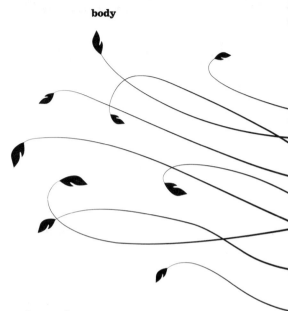

'The food you eat can either be the safest and most powerful form of medicine or the slowest form of poison.'

Ann Wigmore

physical activity

For so many of us, 'exercise' is simply a tool to work off what we ate the day before. We use it to keep our body fat in check and our bikini bodies in shape or we avoid it altogether. However, physical activity is a powerful way to keep both body and mind healthy – and for keeping us alive longer too.

Studies have found that people who do not exercise have the highest risk of premature death, whereas even a little activity can make a big difference, with about thirty minutes a day offering significant health benefits. Building in regular daily movement, even something as simple as walking, can improve your health exponentially.

Physical activity also increases serotonin and dopamine production, which are the feel-good chemicals that make us feel happier. So, besides benefitting our bodies, exercise improves mood, lowers stress and can play a role in preventing mental health issues.

'FOOD is the most abused anxiety drug. EXERCISE is the most underutilised antidepressant.'

Bill Phillips, *Body for Life*

make it easy to exercise

We all lead busy lives in which many things are vying for our attention, and we'll often choose the path of least resistance if this makes things easier for us. The same is true for exercise. The more convenient and easier we make it, the more likely we are to stick to our routine.

If your diary is always busy and you find you can't commit to exercise after work, consider lunchtimes or mornings. If, for instance, you're someone who prefers to exercise in the morning, have your exercise clothes and trainers ready so you fall out of bed and into them.

Pick a running route, gym or exercise class that's near work or home so you don't have to travel too far to get there. (My gym was opposite my workplace for years so that when I left the building, instead of turning right to the station, all I had to do was turn left to hit the gym.)

Get creative! Do something you LOVE to do so that exercise doesn't feel like a chore.

create a movement menu

Think about all the ways you move your body that make you feel good, strong and capable. It might be sex (yes, that counts!), sports, running, yoga, Pilates, ice skating, rock climbing, ballroom dancing, walking the dog, hiking, swimming – the list is endless.

There isn't just one way to exercise, irrespective of what you might see on Instagram, so choose to do things that you enjoy and look forward to. In fact, the word 'exercise' itself can be really off-putting for some of us, which is why I prefer to think of it as 'physical activity' or just 'movement'.

Compile a list of all the ways you move your body that you enjoy. This is your movement menu.

Then start to explore all the opportunities in your local area, both at home and work, where you might be able to do the things on your menu.

Et voilà! – you now have a working menu from which, on any given day, you can pick a variety of ways to move your body that make you feel amazing.

work out
with a friend

It's true what they say – things are better shared. It's often easier to commit to something when you know someone else is depending on you. Working out with a friend is also great for motivation and moral support. Taking your first class or gym session is a lot less scary the first time if you have someone you know and trust by your side.

keep it real

The number one reason people fall off the exercise wagon is because they go for an 'all or nothing' type approach. In the Mind part of this book, we looked at all-or-nothing thinking and the reasons why it sets you up for failure (see page 24 if you want to scoot back and remind yourself). It's almost always better to start small and establish a realistic routine that you can build on.

So, if you know you've a busy week or month ahead, or you're just starting to get into a physical-activity routine, be honest and practical: how much time can you really commit to – and I mean *really* commit to?

If you set yourself up for inevitable success – that is, aiming for what you absolutely know you'll be able to commit to when you first set out – you'll feel better about yourself and what you've achieved, and you're more likely to build on it.

So, block your exercise time out as a meeting in your diary. This is an appointment with yourself: honour it.

listen to your body

There are definitely times when our bodies need rest. In fact, if you're regularly working out, one of the single most important things you need to do is to rest your body so that it can repair, recover and grow. Many of us are so busy ticking things off our schedule and 'to-do' list that we forget to listen to what our bodies actually need.

There might be days when you're exhausted, feeling unwell or, frankly, just need to curl up at home under the covers. There's no shame or gain from pushing your body through a workout when all you need is rest; in fact you're more likely to do yourself harm than good.

There are also days where you're just looking for an excuse to opt out, but when actually moving your body will do you the world of good. Learn to slow down enough to listen to what your body really needs – and respect it.

how to exercise when you travel or when you're busy

Let's face it, many of us have inconsistent routines, periods of oh-my-God-how-the-hell-am-I-going-survive-this, and days when we simply don't come up for air. But here's the thing – making YOU a priority is your priority, because if you burn out, crash out or pass out, the person who really suffers most is you. Make time for the important things like exercise because if you're healthy, well and feeling good, you'll perform better in every other area of your life.

Here are some easy wins for when you're busy or travelling:

❋ Do an online exercise class in your bedroom. (See the Self Care Toolkit, page 204, for some online classes that I love.)

❋ Go for a brisk walk round the block.

❋ Check out the local parks, gyms and yoga studios – many do thirty-minute classes.

❋ Remember that physical activity includes biking, walking and hiking – not just time in the gym or in your running gear.

❋ Stay in one of the increasing chains of health and fitness hotels, which have workout equipment in the bedroom and running routes, gyms and exercise facilities available around the clock.

❋ Do some functional exercises in your room (such as lunges, squats, press-ups).

❋ Do a HIIT workout – HIIT stands for 'high-intensity interval training'. (Note:

true HIIT workouts are only a few minutes long and you'll want to have a lie down afterwards.)

build physical activity into your every day

We tend to lead sedentary lifestyles in the modern age, so building physical activity into our every day is an easy way to increase our exercise levels without even thinking about it.

With new research recommending we do thirty minutes of activity a day, we could all benefit from getting more movement into our daily routines. Here are some simple and quick ways to do just that:

※ Squat whilst you're waiting for the kettle to boil. (Thanks for this tip, Jackie Wren!)

❋ Do 20 pelvic floor exercises every time you go to the toilet, just put the seat down first! (Another great tip from Jackie.)

❋ Take the stairs instead of the lift.

❋ Get off a stop early on the way to work and on the way home.

❋ Bike or walk to work.

❋ Stand up to take phone calls.

❋ Take a walk at lunchtime.

❋ Buy a fitness tracker and track your steps to take 10,000 a day.

❋ Meet friends in the park and go for a walk or play a sports game.

❋ Go and see a colleague rather than email them.

❋ Add ten minutes on to a dog walk.

❋ Walk (or even power walk!) to do your errands, rather than drive.

❋ Incorporate a HIIT workout into your day.

'Your body is designed to move and move regularly. You don't need an expensive gym or yoga studio or fancy sportswear to move your body and feel the benefits. Just get moving.'

Jackie Wren, Personal Trainer and Co-Creator of Davina McCall Fitness DVDs

set yourself a challenge

Having a goal can really help to motivate you and keep you committed to your fitness, whether it's running a marathon or your first 5k; doing a triathlon or a bike ride; going on a hike or a trek; or maybe even committing to going to yoga or another class for thirty days straight.

It doesn't matter how big or small you may think your goal is: by setting one to work towards, you're much more likely to get up and out even on bad days. Having goals like these work for many reasons, one of the biggest being a sense of social accountability. When we publically state we're working towards something, we're far more likely to strive to achieve it. We also want to feel we're progressing and working towards something meaningful in the eyes of others.

beauty sleep

Our relationship with sleep is vital for our overall wellbeing, yet often overlooked. While we might measure our strength, ability and even our output by how little sleep we need, sleep deprivation has been used as a form of torture for years. And many of us now torture ourselves on a daily basis by assuming we can make do with less of it.

There are various scientific theories about why we need sleep. One key role of sleep is to help us process and store memories, with brain scans of sleeping people showing how our brains 'consolidate' or move pieces of information from the short-term memory into the long-term memory. When we sleep, our bodies are also repairing and restoring muscles and tissues, as well as synthesising hormones, which is vital for our body to function properly.

It's important to sleep well if you want to live well.

'I have one piece of advice for you, sleep your way to the top.'
Arianna Huffington, *Thrive*

the magic of sleep

So what happens when you sleep?

The body's circadian rhythm is a natural biological process and part of the cycle is the 'sleep–wake' cycle, according to which we're designed to sleep when it's dark and be awake when it's light.

Sleep itself occurs in ninety minute cycles, split into four parts. Initially, we feel drowsy and move into light sleep. This is often called 'true sleep' and makes up around 50 per cent of a night's sleep, when the body slows down, blood pressure drops and breathing slows.

We then move into 'slow wave' sleep, followed by the 'deep sleep' stage – and this is when the body works its magic. A critical part of the sleep cycle, it's when the growth hormone is secreted and our bodies repair and grow, renewing

skin cells and fighting the free radicals that
can cause things like cancer. And it's when our
metabolism, hormones and appetite are regulated.
During deep sleep, our brain detoxifies itself when
cerebrospinal fluid flows through its channels.

Finally, we move into the REM stage of
sleep. This is where our heart rate and blood
pressure rise and our limbs become paralysed
as we move into a dream state. This is when our
memories are processed and moved from our
short-term memory into our long-term memory.

sleep deprived?

So what happens if we don't get enough sleep?

Studies show that a lack of sleep can impact
on health, mental wellbeing and productivity.
Besides adversely affecting individuals, sleep
deprivation can have negative consequences for
society as a whole.

Specifically, people with insomnia suffer from greater levels of depression and anxiety than those who sleep normally. There are physical risks too. In the UK, one in five traffic accidents are caused by fatigue. Not to mention the economic costs; employees with insomnia cost USA industry billions of dollars each year.

Here are a few key indicators to help you tell if you're sleep deprived:

* Suffering from a foggy brain, poor concentration or difficulty focusing.
* Putting on weight and craving carbohydrates and/or sugar.
* Getting frequent coughs, colds and bugs.
* Constantly hitting the snooze button when you wake up.

If you have one or more of these symptoms it's worth taking a look at your sleep pattern! For optimum health, make a good night's sleep part of your daily self care routine.

ban tech from the bedroom

Many of us are guilty of taking tech to bed. If you bring your devices into the bedroom, this is your wakeup call.

Our bodies are naturally programmed to respond to light levels and, as the night draws in, we naturally start to produce melatonin, making us drowsy and ready for sleep. However, the blue light emitted by devices, like smartphones and tablets, can suppress the production of melatonin, making us feel more awake and it harder to sleep. Likewise, if in the night you get notifications and alerts that cause your screen to light up, your body responds to the light and starts to bring you out of sleep.

This sort of sleep interference doesn't just impact on our sleep cycles but our health too. Melatonin has a key role to play in our circulatory system, and, if there is less melatonin in our system, it's been shown to increase the risk of heart disease, stroke, type two diabetes, depression and dementia, as well as a host of other illnesses.

So put your tech in another room and buy an old-fashioned alarm clock or a wake-up light – and use it as an excuse to get up every morning without pressing snooze!

create a luxurious bedtime routine

We treat ourselves to many things, facials, spas, holidays, manicures, so why not make sleep a luxurious treat?

Set up a regular routine to let your body know it's time for sleep. Some things you could consider are:

* Turning down the lights.
* Turning off your tech.
* Having a bath.
* Lighting some candles.
* Reading a book.
* Buying beautiful bedtime clothes that feel luxurious and special.
* Playing relaxing music.
* Putting lavender on your pillow.

Use sleep as an opportunity for some pampering time and see it as part of your daily self care.

listen to your body

As we saw on page 123, our bodies follow a natural rhythm that is sensitive to light levels. This circadian rhythm is found in all other mammals; however, humans are the only ones that are thought to delay sleep deliberately.

Try not to do this. If you're tired, curl up and get some shut eye. If you can, and it's not too late in the afternoon to disturb your sleep at night, have a snooze. Short naps have been shown to improve mood, alertness and performance – but be warned, they don't make up for loss of a good night's sleep.

light therapy alarm clocks

Winter can really disrupt our sleep cycles and overall sense of wellbeing. Seasonal Affective Disorder is believed to affect about 10 to 20 per cent of people, while four out of six of us are thought to suffer from some form of winter depression.

Light therapy has been shown to have significant benefits. Buying a wakeup light (of which there are many brands and options available) not only helps you wake up naturally but it's a much nicer and gentler way to come to your senses than with an alarm. Wakeup lights also simulate the sunlight that's often missing in winter months, which is why they're so effective for treating winter depression.

'Fall in love with bedtime, when you close your eyes so much magic happens.'
**Rachel McGuinness,
The 'Go-To Sleep' expert**

your bedroom should be for sleep and sex only... (you can thank me later)

Your bedroom is a sanctuary.

Keep it tidy, free of distractions (such as work, tech, TV and mess) and make it a space for rest and recuperation.

If you must use it for more than one purpose, aim to have a screen, partition or other way of separating the space so you get the full benefit when it's used as a bedroom.

self care takeaway tips

❋ Learn to love the miraculous body you've got, focus on the things that make you special unique and, yes, beautiful!

❋ Get to know your personal eating habits and let healthy eating become an easy and consistent lifestyle – not a regime.

❋ Enjoy your food – make mealtimes fun, ditch diets and ban the scales!

❋ Find a form of physical activity you love and make it a part of your daily life.

❋ Prioritise your sleep and ban tech from the bedroom.

life

'Go confidently in the direction of your dreams! Live the life you imagined.'

Henry David Thoreau

Attributed to the American writer Thoreau and based on his classic book *Walden*, the quote this section begins with has been on my bedroom wall – and now my office wall – for most of my life.

Whenever we discuss our lives, our hopes and our dreams, most of us skirt around the fact that our time is finite – and none of us know when it's going to end. It's sad that it often takes a death, cancer or tragedy with a capital T to remind us how lucky we are and to appreciate the important things in life.

My challenge to you is not to wait until you're forced to discover this – choose today, right now, to live fully. Embrace life as a gift. Dance like no one is watching. Pull out the 'good sheets' and use them. Wear your best clothes to the supermarket if the mood strikes you. Dream big. And fight for the dreams you believe in.

Don't wait for 'permission' or the 'perfect conditions' – they'll never arrive; all we ever have is *now*. This section of the book is designed to inspire you to live YOUR extraordinary life.

conduct a life audit

The important areas of life typically fall into eight broad categories:

* Health and wellbeing
* Relationships
* Career
* Fun and leisure
* Personal growth
* Money
* Spirituality
* Physical environment

As we saw in the 'Mind' section, life can get busy, and balance is about understanding that at different times in our life different aspects need to take priority. Every six months or so, sit down and look at the key areas of your life: where are things going well? What areas need a bit more attention or focus? What areas might be suffering because your attention is on other things? Where does the balance need to be redressed? In the Self Care Toolkit, on page 206, you'll find an exercise called the Wheel of Life, which is an effective and easy tool to help complete this exercise.

Remember, it's OK for things to move and change. Sometimes you'll need to focus on your career, which might mean family and fun take a backseat for a while. Likewise, you might need to prioritise family time for a while, and put your career on hold.

Life is a journey that changes just like a river flows. There is no such thing as the 'perfect balance', only honouring the priorities you have in the here and now. All you can do is make mindful and conscious decisions to create the perfect balance for you at that time.

be clear about where you're going and why

Goals are wishes with plans. Often the simple act of stating our plans and desires to the world can make it more likely we'll go out and achieve them. When, aged ten, I announced in my geography class that I'd see the Amazon jungle one day, I had no idea how – I just knew I would. Eighteen years later, I finally landed in Ecuador.

We're also much more likely to achieve our goals if we write them down. It's such a simple yet powerful act. When designing your goals, make them as specific as you can: 'I want to save £100' is a much more meaningful and clear statement than 'I want to save more'.

Equally, putting a time frame in place can help us focus and plan ahead. Depending on whether you need to save £100 by the end of the month or £100 by the end of the year, the likelihood is the two options will lead to different actions and plans.

Make your goals *exciting*: we all want to do things that mean something to us, that excite us and stimulate us. The 'why' behind the goal is just as important as the goal itself, because this is what motivates us and keeps us on track even on those days when we want to veer off course. While saving £100 is great, for instance, being clear you're saving £100 to buy a flight to meet your niece for the first time is a much more compelling motive and means you're more likely to achieve your goal.

But what if you find it hard to know what you want? Or what if asking for what you want just doesn't come easy? In the Self Care Toolkit on page 208, I've shared a beautiful exercise to help you connect to what you really want – and it starts with your eightieth birthday.

managing stress – don't sweat the small stuff

We've already seen the impact stress can have on our bodies. While a degree of stress can help us perform at our best, being subjected to constant pressures can damage our health and wellbeing in many ways. In fact, learning how to manage our stress levels is invaluable if we want to have the energy to focus on the things that matter most.

Here are five tips for coping with stress:

1. Ask yourself if it will matter a year from now

We often perceive the current situation or moment we're in to be more dramatic or life impacting than it really is. But if we were to fast-forward to a year from now, the likelihood is we wouldn't even remember this episode.

2. Control the controllables

Life is complex. We can't control all our experiences, so learning to let go and focus on the things we can control will make managing the tricky stuff easier. For example, we can't always control whether we're going to fall ill. But we can control what we eat, how frequently we take physical activity, how often we have health checks, and the vaccines we get when we go on holiday. Likewise, we can't control what people think of us, but we can control how we behave, the quality of our work, the kind of friend we are and how we present ourselves. Remember, we can always control our attitude, the effort we put into something and how we respond to situations.

3. Ask for help

So many of us don't want to bother our friends or family. At work, we don't want to appear like we can't cope. At home, we want our partners or kids to magically understand that we're struggling without our having to say anything. Asking for help isn't a sign of weakness; it's a critical part of self care, accepting that we can't do it all on our own. It also allows others to understand exactly how they can help, which can enhance many relationships. Imagine how you've felt in the past when you've witnessed a friend or loved one struggle, and felt powerless to help. If, for instance, they'd said, 'You know what, I'd love some help with this project' or 'I'd just like a hug now and then' – wouldn't you have jumped to their aid and felt like you were doing good?

4. Take a break

When we're in the middle of a stressful situation
it can be hard to see all the options we have.
Taking a break can give us the space, time and
distance we need to calm our nervous system,
increase productivity and creativity, and see the
situation more clearly. If your baby is screaming,
your project deadlines are looming, the boss is
being a nightmare – whatever the problem is –
try to get outside and walk around the block and
just breathe. The sunlight, exercise and fresh air
will all do wonders for you, and the space will
give you the opportunity to think.

5. Breathe!

The simple act of breathing is one of the most
beneficial and essential tools we have for self care.
It calms our minds, nervous systems and brings
fresh oxygen into the body. It replenishes and
invigorates us. When we're in a stressful situation,
taking some calming breaths and filling our lungs

and body with fresh air (as shared in the Mind section, page 49) will help calm your nervous system, clear your head and relax your body.

less is more – the power of slow

In our modern, fast-paced world, so many of us spend our lives running about and squeezing multiple things into a day to feel productive. Yet we miss the magic of life when we rush through our days and we can forget to be grateful for the magical things that happen. When we constantly push for 'what's next' we tend to forget 'what is'.

Consider these tips to help you connect to slow:

❋ Look up next time you're walking to work: you'll notice lots of buildings and interesting details that you haven't seen before, or you might just notice the clouds and beauty in the sky.

* Eat your meals slowly at a table set away from distractions.
* When you take part in a conversation, listen to *hear* – not just for your chance to respond.
* Start a daily gratitude practice or make your own daily record of things that make you happy (for more ideas on gratitude, see page 43).
* Give yourself the time you need to make appointments without rushing.

celebrate regularly

When you're climbing a mountain, it's easy to only keep looking up to see how far you have to go. Instead, we all need to become better at appreciating where we are – and remember to look behind now and then to see how far we've come! That's not to say it isn't good to keep your eye on the prize, but remember that the journey itself has a lot to teach you. When you get that promotion, celebrate it. Spend time with people you love on your birthday and celebrate the fact you're a year older (every year is a gift!). Celebrate when you run your first mile or when you land a new client or when you conquer a fear.

It's so easy to overlook achievements and focus on 'what's next?' or 'how can I do better?' When we celebrate our wins regularly we reinforce the message that we're progressing, achieving and moving forward, which motivates us to continue.

❋ Try starting your weekly appraisals with what's going well.
❋ When a friend next asks how you are, share a success story.

✳ When you go to a networking event or meeting, share a win.

✳ When you reach a milestone you've set yourself, treat yourself to something – whether that's a glass of champagne, a new book, a facial, time with loved ones or something entirely different.

✳ Keep a success journal, capturing every success as it happens and then review it at the end of each month.

✳ Have a celebration buddy with whom you can celebrate your wins.

connection

Human beings crave connection. We look for connections in the form of relationships and friendships, and also in our surroundings. We want to feel comfortable, at home and like we belong.

Fitting in and belonging were crucial to our survival back in the Stone Age, when we were hunter-gatherers. If we were rejected by our tribe, there was a danger we'd be left behind and our chances of survival were slim. While we've evolved in many ways, the need for belonging and connection is a constant factor in human behaviour.

What does connection mean to you?

connection with our friends

In our always-on world, where the other side of the planet is only a push of a button away, where we can share every thought, moment and idea on the internet, and we're never separated by more than a 'like' or WhatsApp from each other, it's a little surprising to find that we're becoming increasingly lonely. I believe this is due to three key reasons.

Firstly, we're not spending our time with the people that matter most or support us best. Secondy, we're often stretched thinly – trying to please too many people – to give the energy and time that our friendships deserve. Finally, we tend to have many more superficial or inauthentic connections with our friends, rather than deep and meaningful relationships. All of these things impact our overall sense of connection.

nurturing friendships

Here are some simple tips you can follow to make sure your friendships flourish:

* Block your schedule so you attend no more than one or two activities a day.
* When you're with friends, instigate a 'no phones' rule and just talk face to face.

❋ Instead of texting or WhatsApping a friend, phone them.

❋ Have a friend cull (no really!). Consider who might be in your life and taking your energy, yet no longer provides a fulfilling friendship. Gently, and with love, allow them to leave your life.

❋ When you get invited to something, do the 'Yes to This, No to That' exercise first (see page 201).

❋ Have a 'first come, first served' rule: whatever you say yes to first stays in the diary (unless it's an emergency or major life event).

❋ Make use of downtime, like traffic jams, to catch up with friends (use your hands-free!).

❋ Join a networking group, or arrange to meet people with similar interests and hobbies if your current friends don't share the same interests as you.

'Friends come into
our lives for a reason,
a season or life.'

romantic relationships

The romantic relationships we enjoy – or don't – can provide vital clues as to how we feel about ourselves. The way we allow other people to treat us says something about what we feel we deserve. As we crave physical intimacy, many people will settle for an unrewarding relationship simply because they fear being alone, or assume they don't deserve better.

Don't ignore the red flags. Be wary of falling in love with the idea rather than the reality.

And don't settle for second best.

Equally, many people put their lives on hold waiting for the 'right one' or the 'perfect person'. They have a list (literally!) of things they want their partner to have or to be, yet they do little or no work to see if they're all they could be themselves.

Cultivating a nourishing and fulfilling relationship means having that relationship

with yourself first. Knowing that you don't
need someone to complete you; rather you need
someone to complement you.

'the one'

And what about when you do find 'the One' –
and settle down?

In a long-term relationship, the people we
love can often get the brunt of our hard day, our
fear, our lack of confidence, our hormonal changes
(ladies!), and we can easily start to take them for
granted. Equally, we might lose ourselves in trying
to please our partner, putting them first in all
situations and never asking for the support, love or
things we need. We can be afraid we might upset
them, frighten them off or worry them, and so we
put aside our own needs to focus on them instead.

Neither of these strategies is a recipe
for a successful relationship. Here are some

suggestions on how to make a relationship work, without losing your sense of self:

1. Make time for each other but also time for you

❋ Set aside one night a week for a date night.

❋ Make dinnertime (or breakfast) your time for each other. Put your phones away and just talk about the day – and really listen.

❋ Give each other space to be alone once in a while: have a bath, read a book, take a walk, work in different rooms, see your friends independently or have independent adventures.

2. Ask for what you need

❋ I hate to break it to you, but none of us are mind readers. If you need more affection, more physical intimacy, someone to take the bins out – don't drop hints, don't get angry, don't build up resentment – just ask

your partner to do it! Be clear about why
you want them to do it, and thank them
when they do.

❋ As and when relationships go through
changes – such as getting married, becoming
parents, career changes or other major life
events – talk about what's expected and the
support you each need. Don't just assume
your partner will know!

3. Know your love language

❋ We each give and receive love in different
ways and have our own 'love language'
which, according to expert Dr Gary
Chapman, is usually based upon five basic
building blocks: Words of Affirmation,
Quality Time, Receiving Gifts, Acts of
Service, and Physical Touch.

❋ Understanding the workings of your own
love language will help you understand how
you need to receive love; while learning

your partner's love language will help you
understand how to give love to them.

※ Take the test together, share your results
and talk about the outcomes (see page 210).

4. *Share your goals but don't be afraid to have your own*

※ Discuss your future plans with your partner
– what key milestones or goals do you share?

※ How can you work together to achieve these
goals and what do you each have to do to
make them a reality?

※ Where do your goals and plans differ and do
these create any challenges for either of you
– if they do, discuss them!

※ How can you support each other to achieve
these independent goals?

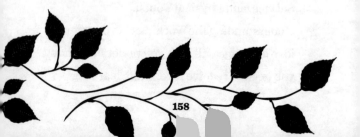

connecting to nature

More and more of us are beginning to appreciate how the natural world offers us an escape from our hectic lives and the chance to unplug from our phones. Not only do food and water nourish our bodies, but sunlight and air do too.

Yet many of us have lost our connection to nature. We live in big cities, ride the subway or tube to work, and spend our days in office blocks with the shutters closed to keep the sun out. We work in square rooms, with square desks and square screens. We have our eyes glued to our smartphones or our ears plugged into iPods... It's little wonder we lose our sense of connection. Hundreds of studies have shown that spending time in nature has many benefits for our mental and physical wellbeing, including:

✳ Reducing depression, anger, anxiety and stress.

✳ Improving mood and self-esteem.

✳ Increasing emotional resilience and energy levels.

✳ Using up excess stress hormones through physical activity.

✳ Building confidence.

For many mental health issues, ecotherapy is a recommended type of treatment. How do you feel after time outdoors?

be natural

In our busy lives, it's still possible to find time to connect to nature. Here are some suggestions to help you reconnect easily with the natural world:

✳ Take a lunchbreak in your local park or green space.

* Get off a stop earlier and walk to work, or cycle there.
* Build a walk into your weekend routine. (Buy or borrow a dog and it's guaranteed!)
* If you have a garden, spend time in it and have fun planting vegetables or herbs.
* Buy flowers or plants for your home.
* Volunteer in a local community project based outdoors.
* Visit your local city farm.
* Consider joining a programme such as 'borrow my dog' to have an excuse to get out and walk – while giving something back to the community at the same time.
* Join a Forest School class.
* Go for a walk with friends instead of going to the pub.
* Build a communal herb garden.
* Get an allotment.
* Have a picnic in the park.
* Go camping instead of clubbing.
* Join an ecotherapy programme.

'When I let go of
what I am, I become
what I might be.'
Lao Tzu

personal growth

Our brains are hardwired to develop and actively seek new opportunities to learn, be that in the context of work, or new experiences, skills and places, or through meeting new people. By opening ourselves up to new ideas, new people, new cultures, skills and opportunities, we feel empowered, invigorated, challenged and alive – which helps us develop as individuals.

For your own personal growth consider exploring one or more of the following:

* Take up (or rediscover) a hobby.
* Travel, whether abroad or at home – there's often exciting places to discover on your doorstep!
* Acquire a new skill.
* Learn a new language.
* Take some training.
* Join a Meet Up group in your area.

✳ Listen to podcasts on a subject that interests you. (Beats the morning news on the commute!)

✳ Read more books and try books on new topics or subjects.

✳ Play a new sport.

contribution

Another way we can grow as people is through contributing to the world around us. You might ask what difference one person can make, but you only have to look at history to find examples of individuals who've made a marked difference. Many of us will already know people in our local community or circle of friends who make a difference – whether it's somebody who volunteers for a homeless charity every Christmas; a friend who rings an old person to chat for an hour each week; the family who planted a community herb garden down the street; or the person who fundraises for charity. There are so many ways to make a difference, from the work we do every day, to the way we treat those around us. Even the smallest gesture, like paying someone a compliment, can lift someone's day.

How could you make a difference?

1. What charity or cause do you feel strongly about?

❋ Could you donate to that charity?

❋ Can you help them fundraise?

❋ Can you get involved in any of their projects?

❋ Could you offer your services in some way?

❋ Could you start your own movement?

2. What life experiences could you share?

❋ What person or group of people could your experiences serve?

❋ Perhaps you could mentor someone?

✳ Or become a spokesperson for a cause?

✳ How about writing a blog about your experiences?

✳ Could you visit a school, a group or a care home to give a talk or make some other use of your skills?

✳ Is there someone in your local community that could use your support?

3. In your place of work:

✳ Who benefits from the work you do?

✳ How do you benefit from your own work?

✳ What does your salary enable you to do?

✳ In what ways do you contribute that make you feel good?

✳ What other opportunities are there to contribute beyond your current role? Perhaps to a network or group or other team?

✳ Is there a company charity you feel passionately about that you could support in some way?

What skills could you use to benefit the company and the customers it serves?

what do you need to let go of?

Our physical world can often give us clues about our internal world. We may hoard physical possessions without realising the impact this has on our psyche and emotional state. Consider those boxes stacked in the garage or loft, the old digital files stored on your computer, the clothes clogging up space in the wardrobe – we all have clutter. By physically clearing space for new things we make changes internally too. Patty Cruz is a professional organiser who says that clearing physical clutter makes way for a more organised, stress-free and productive life. According to Patty, being organised is not about having a minimalist environment, or living and working in a space that looks like a spread from an interior's magazine; it's about 'finding your things when you need them, being calm and happy in your environment and having time and energy to spend it on what really matters to you'.

Did you know that clutter negatively affects your ability to focus and increases your stress levels? However, an uncluttered environment will enhance your ability to focus and to be efficient!

decluttering

When decluttering, jump in the deep end and start with the area that bothers you the most – the one that makes you feel most stuck. This is the space that will have the most impact on you, your life and your ability to focus. Patty suggests you ask yourself these three questions:

✳ What is my vision?

✳ Why am I doing this?

✳ What does the ideal situation look and
   feel like?

Being clear about your vision will help you to
decide what to keep and what to let go. You won't
be clearing out just for the sake of it, because
you are expected to, or because decluttering is
all the rage. Your vision will be your driver, your
GPS, and by taking time to step back and really
think about the nature of that vision, you'll know
instinctively which belonging, activity or person
aligns with it. Then you'll have greater clarity and
letting go of things that don't fit your vision will
become far easier to do.

personal appearance

How many of us have clothes we keep for sentimental reasons, or because we're hoping we'll fit back into them one day, or because it frankly feels like too much effort to sort through them and throw them out? And how many of us open the wardrobe each morning and think 'I've nothing to wear!' despite the wardrobe bursting at the seams?

Most of us would agree that when we look good and take care in our appearance, we feel good too. Which means there's a lot to be said for having a regular clothes review as a way to make sure your clothes represent your best you.

Image consultant Lizzie Edwards recommends taking the following five steps to update your wardrobe:

1.   Create a style-inspiration board full of pictures of things that you love and find

aesthetically pleasing – from locations, to food, to architecture. This will give you an insight into your personal style, the colour you like and your taste.

2.   Then have a thorough clear out of your wardrobe. Whatever you keep should be either practical or loved. The fewer clothes in the wardrobe, the easier it will be to wear something you love every day.

3.   Don't save things for best: every day is all we have, so dress down smarter items and wear them on the school run, to Sunday lunch or to the pub. Get wear out of the things you love!

4.   Buy matching hangers so your wardrobe looks organised and getting dressed is a much nicer experience. Hang up as much as possible, ordering your clothes by item and colour, starting with black through to white.

5.   Let go of things you've been holding on to for sentimental reasons. If it was something gifted to you, remember the gift is in the

giving, and if it's not 'you', let it go. Pass on the gift or donate it to charity where it can continue to bring someone else pleasure. For highly sentimental items, store them separately in a special box, or take a photo of them and then let them go. Your memories are not sown into the garment and a picture can hold as much sentimental value as the item itself.

The best wardrobe is one where, when you open it, everything is an option – it's clean, it fits, and it's for the right season, ready to go.

financial self care

Is money a part of self care? Absolutely! Many of us grew up hearing phrases like 'money is the root of all evil', or 'money doesn't grow on trees', or 'rich people are greedy'. It's said we'd rather talk about sex than money. Yet money is a factor in almost every aspect of our lives, including our mental wellbeing, with money worries often contributing to stress and anxiety. Interestingly, our relationship with money can often be a reflection of how we're treating ourselves. For example:

* You might feel unworthy and 'not good enough' – which is more likely to mean you won't ask for a pay raise.
* If you are someone who binges on food, it's highly likely you will also binge-buy clothes to get a short-term 'high'.
* You might feel undeserving of good things, so you're more likely not to invest in yourself.
* If you have a tendency to bury your head in the sand about challenges, it's likely you'll have debts or responsibilities you don't want to face.

So how do you start looking after your financial self care?

work on your money beliefs

We all have beliefs about money that will impact, either directly or indirectly, how we earn our money and what we do with it. As we've seen, these beliefs often stem from our upbringing, the society we live in and how we saw our parents and siblings interact with money. You may, for example, have a belief that being economically successful (or rich) is somehow not spiritual, or that it's greedy and wrong to care about money. Yet the Dalai Lama says, 'Money is good. It is important. Without it daily survival – not to mention further development – is impossible.' Perhaps you believe you have to 'work hard for money', so you do work hard, putting in extra hours at the office and taking on extra jobs. Yet many of the wealthiest people say they learned to make money work for them by investing and using their finances wisely.

Consider what your beliefs around money are by completing these sentences:

✳ Money is _____ .

✳ Money means _____ .

✳ I'd love to have more money but

_____ .

These three questions can reveal a LOT about your feelings concerning money. Consider how the beliefs that they reveal might be impacting on the ways you make or spend money. Do they empower you and help you? Make you fearful or nervous? Create a balanced view of money? Do they reflect how you spend money?

In the Self Care Toolkit, on page 211, you will find an exercise to help you start turning these money beliefs around.

declutter your money world

As we saw earlier, decluttering our homes and wardrobes can help us improve our focus, energy, mood and creativity. Decluttering our money world has the same benefits – plus the potential to save us money, restructure our finances and boost our income. Here are four different decluttering exercises you can do TODAY:

1. Collect all the loose change you have lying around the house

Gather up all those coins stashed in pots, cupboards, drawers, pockets, car ashtrays or under the sofa, and take your loot to the bank where you can change it up into big notes. Then treat yourself to something fun and nice. Enjoy spending it. This goes for gift cards too (unless you're saving them for something specific, of course). Did you know the amount of unused credit on UK gift cards comes to around £300 million each year?

2. Clear out your wallet

Think about this. If you took out your wallet and looked at it, what would it say about your relationship with money? Is it organised and clear of old receipts? Crowded and cluttered? Tattered and old and barely holding things together? If it is, go and give it a clean out, or buy a new one!

3. Clear out your old bank accounts

Do you have any dormant bank accounts? How about old direct debits that don't need to be in place anymore? Do you need to merge your debt into one 0 per cent card? Do you even check your balance regularly? Allocate some time to review your bank statements properly, and make sure the payments are up to date. While this might take some time to achieve, it'll be a HUGE relief when it's done.

4. Do a money audit

Where do you spend your money? Are you saving the amount you want to save each month? Are your spending habits creating problems, or are they working towards your goals and values?

A great way to track this is by setting up a money-tracking app that links to your bank account(s) and then schedule some time each week to sit down and review your spend. Ask yourself if you're spending your money in the best way possible and what changes you might need to make to better meet your goals.

get a financial advisor

There's never a right or wrong time to see a financial advisor, but I'd go so far as to say the best time was ten years ago, and the second-best time is now. Working with somebody who can help you plan ahead and invest your money wisely will give you the best possible chance of meeting your lifestyle and money goals.

If you can't afford to work with a financial advisor, there are many great websites that offer practical advice and ideas, which can be a good place to start. (Check the Self Care Toolkit on page 210 for some suggested websites.)

get practical – set up a budget

With an increasing number of people in debt, it's clear many of us are living beyond our means. If that includes you, there's no better time than now to sit down and get practical. What you'll need:

   Your pay cheque.

✳ Any other income statements for the month (such as rent coming in from property, assets, second job etc.).

✳ Your bank statement(s).

✳ Your bills and outgoings (credit card bills, tax, water, gas, electric, etc.).

✳ A pen, paper and a calculator / Excel spreadsheet.

Sit down and work out what your household income is each month. Then work out what your monthly outgoings are. How much do you have left each month? If you have a surplus, that's brilliant: is it enough to meet your lifestyle and money goals? If you have a deficit, consider what areas you could reduce or cut, what bills you could pay off, what companies you could switch or combine to save money each month. Often, even small changes can have a big impact; for example, cutting out a £2 cup of coffee every day could save you over £50 a month.

If you find you're struggling with debt, seek help and don't suffer in silence. There are many independent agencies and companies out there to support people in debt, and many options that could potentially support you.

have a five-year and a ten-year plan

Many financial experts, including the brains behind misslolly.com, talk of the benefits of having a five- and ten-year plan. How can you know what to save or invest today if you don't know where you're heading? Sort out your priorities. If you couldn't care less about cars, then saving for a convertible is never going to make you go that extra mile with your financial planning. To be in control Miss Lolly says you should be able to answer the following questions:

✳ When would you like to have enough
savings in the bank so you could retire if
you wanted to? How much would you need
in today's money to live the life you want on
retirement?

✳ What's the next property step for you?
Whether you are moving up the ladder or
getting on it for the first time, you need to
know when is the right time to make your
move, how much it will cost to buy or rent,
and how much your home will cost you
per month.

Once you have worked out these plans, build
on them. What about saving for a holiday of a
life time? A little nest egg for a rainy day?
Helping the kids through university? How about
extending your home? It's never too soon to plan
for the future.

self care takeaway tips

✳ Set yourself some goals and conduct
a regular life audit to keep yourself
focussed on your priorities and goals.

✳ Celebrate your wins.

✳ Connect more deeply and meaningfully
to your friends and loved ones.

✳ Take time out in nature to revitalise
your body as well as your mind.

✳ Declutter your home, your wardrobe and
your finances.

✳ Be committed to your own personal
growth and development.

conclusion: self care for life

My biological father died when I was just eighteen months old. My mum remarried the most wonderful man you can imagine, who raised me as his own, proving you don't need to be genetically related to be an incredible parent. However, it is only as I've grown older that I've realised my father's death has been a driving force throughout my life. His death at the age of only thirty-six taught me the importance of living passionately and embracing every opportunity.

Surviving eating disorders, burn out and bullying has given me first-hand experience of what a lack of self love and self care can lead to. I feel I cheated myself in so many ways when I think back to all the moments I missed, opportunities I turned down and people I hurt as a result of my illness and the way I felt about myself. But it's also given me a unique and privileged opportunity to see a different perspective, to understand how amazing our bodies really are and what they're capable of when we nourish them rather than punish them.

Hopefully by now you can see self care isn't something you do on ad-hoc days, or just on the bad days, or when you have enough money to do things. It's not about bubble baths or facials (although they're lovely treats). Self care is the everyday commitment you make to yourself to look after and treat yourself with the love and respect you deserve.

So, whilst this is my story, it's really YOUR story. This is part of your journey, too, which is why you're here. Love yourself fiercely, not because I tell you to or because it's on a Yoga t-shirt, but because you – just as you are, right here, right now – are an amazing miracle. Commit to nourishing yourself and making YOU your priority.

'Self care is for life: go live it.'

self care for when you're having a really crap day

Let's face it, some days are just 'bleh' and with the best intentions in the world we can end up feeling crap, be down about ourselves and quickly fall into bad habits. These fifty tips cover all aspects of mind, body and life for when the crap days hit and you need an instant self care boost:

1. Call your best friend.
2. Put on your feel-good song or a song that lights you up (and dance if the mood takes you).
3. Start your day with lemon and water.
4. Buy yourself flowers.
5. Smile.
6. Pay someone a compliment.
7. Take twenty minutes to sit in nature.
8. Change your password for your PC to something motivational.
9. Drink an extra glass of water.
10. Swap a chocolate bar for a piece of fruit, or a coffee for a mint tea.
11. Find a quote that motivates you and make it your home screen.
12. Write down three things you're grateful for right now.
13. Go for a walk around the block.
14. Take an exercise class (even a thirty-minute speed class).

15. Do three simple stretches.

16. Unplug all your devices for an hour, switch off and just relaaaaaax...

17. Listen to a guided meditation.

18. Throw away your newspaper and listen to a podcast on your commute home.

19. Watch a comedy sketch on YouTube by your favourite comedian.

20. Simplify things for yourself today by focussing on the essentials.

21. Cancel your plans tonight, and go home and relax.

22. Plan to be in bed by 9 p.m.

23. Read a chapter of your favourite book.

24. Cook your favourite meal.

25. Try a new food or recipe.

26. Do a simple breathing exercise for five minutes.

27. List ten things you've achieved that you're proud of.

28. Do something just for fun.

29. Declutter your handbag or work desk.
30. Get fifteen minutes of daylight.
31. Go watch the clouds.
32. Write out your thoughts, then bin or burn them to let them go.
33. Ask for help.
34. Make one of your meals as colourful as you can.
35. Wear your favourite piece of clothing or jewellery.
36. Take five minutes to look through old photos.
37. Read positive feedback or statements about yourself.
38. Give your body a treat.
39. Hang out with a friend who radiates love and positivity.
40. Grab a massage or facial.
41. Repeat a positive affirmation.
42. Book in an adventure (even if it's just taking a new bus or route to work!).
43. Get off a stop early and walk to work or home.

44. Sit quietly for ten minutes.

45. Every time you go to the loo, when you've finished put the seat down and do twenty pelvic-floor exercises. (You'll easily reach the hundred a day recommended by personal trainers!)

46. Pet an animal.

47. Take a bike ride.

48. Let go of something.

49. Say no to something in order to say yes to yourself.

50. Get a hug from someone you love.

the self care toolkit

All worksheets and exercise are available to download at melnoakes.com/book

mind

Mental Health Organisations

While I don't endorse or recommend any specifically, here are the website details of some independent bodies and charities based in the UK, USA and Australia that offer support for mental health conditions.

UK

* Beat – b-eat.co.uk
* Child and Adolescent Mental Health – youngminds.org.uk/find-help/your-guide-to-support/guide-to-camhs
* Mental Health Foundation – mentalhealth.org.uk
* Mind – mind.org.uk
* NHS – nhs.uk
* Sane – sane.org.uk
* Samaritans – samaritans.org

USA

* American Mental Health Foundation – americanmentalhealthfoundation.org
* Anxiety and Depression Association of America – adaa.org
* Mental Health America – mentalhealthamerica.net
* NAMI – nami.org

Australia

✳ Beyond Blue – beyondblue.org.au

✳ CAN – canmentalhealth.org.au

✳ Grow – grow.org.au

✳ Headspace – headspace.org.au

✳ Sane – sane.org

Meeting your 'Inner Critic'

Close your eyes and tune into the voices that tell you you're not good enough. It might be uncomfortable, we're so used to battling the voice that allowing it 'free reign' can feel a little intimidating. That's ok. Give yourself permission to just listen for a few moments and complete the chart on the next page.

My 'Inner Critic'
My inner critic's name is
It usually shows up when
Its secret fear is
It takes the shape of
I notice the voice
The voice belongs to
Its favourite sayings and stories are
It speaks
It makes me feel
I also notice

When you have this information you're much more able to distinguish 'you' from 'it' and so you can more easily communicate with it and turn down the volume when you need to.

Positive Affirmations

Check www.melnoakes.com/book to download a cheat sheet of 40 of my favourite positive affirmations.

Thought Log

A thought log is a method used in Cognitive Behavioural Therapy (CBT). This powerful tool will help you understand how your thoughts and behaviours are linked. It allows you to start noticing the negative thoughts you have, often automatically, and enables you to examine the evidence and choose a different response that might be more realistic in the circumstances. Fill it in whenever you find yourself struggling in a situation or recurring type of situation.

Situation / Event	[Example:] I made a mistake at work
Thoughts	I'm such an idiot, I always mess things up
Feelings	Feel like a failure
Behaviours / actions	I cried in the toilet
Evidence that supports this thought	My boss was upset and I made the mistake
Evidence that doesn't support this thought	It's the first mistake I made at work
Alternative thought	I tried my best. I learned a valuable lesson.

Yes to This, No to That

This exercise enables you to say 'no' with grace and ease. It's not about passing judgment or pointing blame; it's simply a quick and effective tool you can use to determine what you want to give your time to.

Yes To This	No To That
e.g. Staying late to finish my work.	e.g. My gym class.
e.g. Meeting a friend for a drink.	e.g. An early night.
e.g. Time for myself.	e.g. Cleaning the house.

Mindfulness and Meditation Apps and Resources

Apps available on Android and IOS

- ❋ Headspace – headspace.com
- ❋ Calm – calm.com
- ❋ Buddhify – buddhify.com
- ❋ Smiling Mind – smilingmind.com.au
- ❋ The Mindfulness App –themindfulnessapp. com
- ❋ Stop, Breathe and Think – app.stopbreathe think.ork/

Online meditation course

chopracentermeditation.com

body

Emotional Hunger vs Physical Hunger

Physical	Emotional
Comes on gradually – you can wait.	Comes on suddenly and feels urgent.
You look for a variety of food.	Has a specific craving, usually involving sugar or carbs (but not always).
Once you're full you can stop eating.	You don't notice you're full, or don't respond to the fullness so eat until you're uncomfortably full.
Feeling satisfied once you've eaten.	Feeling guilty once you've eaten.
You feel it in your stomach.	You think it in your head.

Food Log – Your Daily Food Diary
This is personal to you and doesn't need to be
shared with anyone else. Please capture honestly
as much of the information listed as possible for
everything you eat. It is important you do this
without judgment or criticism of yourself!

Online Classes I Love
Here are the details of some online exercise
classes that I've enjoyed. I hope you will get a lot
out of them too:
* youtube.com/user/blogilates
* sweatybetty.com/free-online-workout-
  videos
* yogaia.com
* fitnessblender.com/videos

Useful online sleep resources
* National Sleep Foundation –
  sleepfoundation.org
* The Sleep Council – sleepcouncil.org.uk

Date: _____

Time	What I ate	Where I ate	Thoughts	Feelings	What I've noticed

life

Wheel of Life

On a scale of 1 to 10 – with 1 being not at all satisfied, and 10 being 100 per cent satisfied – go around the wheel and mark yourself in each area.

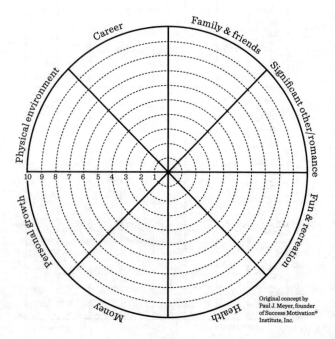

Original concept by
Paul J. Meyer, founder
of Success Motivation®
Institute, Inc.

When you're finished, draw a line between the dots. Then ask yourself:

※ Which areas of the wheel are calling out for the most attention?

※ Which dots are where I want them to be? How do I keep them there?

※ Which dots are not where I want them to be and what do I need to do to change that?

※ Which am I surprised about?

※ Which area do I need to integrate more into my life?

※ What do I need to do to nourish myself in that area?

Goal Setting:

※ Specific – what exactly do you want?

※ Measurable – how will you know when you've reached your goal?

※ Achievable – can you achieve the goal in the time you have?

※ Realistic – is it a realistic goal?

✳ Timely – by when do you want to have achieved this?

✳ Exciting – what's the why behind the why?

✳ Relevant – does this fit into your life?

Visualisation: Your Eightieth Birthday

Sit or lie somewhere comfortable. Close your eyes and take some deep breaths. With each breath, imagine your body relaxing and softening into the seat or bed. Feel your muscles relax and your breathing becoming deeper. Now take yourself forward in the timeline of your life.

You're at your eightieth birthday party surrounded by the people you care about the most. There's cake (there's always cake!) and candles. The space is filled with love and you start to recount the story of your life. Visualise the space: are you inside or outside? Sitting or standing? What are you wearing? What can you hear? Smell? Feel?

Picture the scene and listen as your own voice starts to recount the story of your life...

✳ Who plays a part in your story?

✳ What have been the key milestones of your life?

✳ What have been your biggest achievements?

✳ What are you most proud of?

✳ What opportunities did you miss that you regret?

✳ What risks did you take that paid off?

✳ What advice would you give your younger self?

✳ What has given you the most joy?

✳ What do you wish you did more of?

✳ What do you want to be remembered for?

Take in all the sights, smells and feelings, and notice what is most important to you in this story of your life. What information do you need to bring back with you? What lessons do you want to learn?

When you're ready to open your eyes, take ten minutes to capture the lessons from the visualisation.

Love Language
Take the test here: 5lovelanguages.com

Financial Advice
While inclusion in this list is not an endorsement of the services they offer, here are the website details of some organisations and websites that offer helpful financial advice:

* Miss Lolly – misslolly.com
* Money Saving Expert – moneysavingexpert. com
* Money Advice Service – moneyadvice service.org.uk
* Your Wealth – yourwealth.co.uk
* Money Supermarket – moneysupermarket. com

Budgeting apps:
* Ontrees – ontrees.com
* Goodbudget – goodbudget.com
* Wally – wally.me
* Money Dashboard – moneydashboard.com

Financial Beliefs

Use this table to discover your beliefs about money, and how you might change your thinking to include more supportive beliefs.

Beliefs I have about money	[Example:] Money is the root of all evil.
Evidence for this belief	Mum and Dad used to fight about money.
How this makes me feel, think and behave	Scared that I'll never have enough money and that I'll argue with my partner.
Why this belief might be incorrect	Money means I can go on holiday and do nice things with friends and do nice things for people.
What belief would be more supportive?	Money is a way to do good in the world

acknowledgments

It's a miraculous thing to turn your passion into words and then see it in print. I am endlessly grateful for all the support, love, encouragement and feedback I've received from my friends, family, clients, peers and everyone who has been on this crazy whirlwind ride with me! In particular, I'd like to thank:

The team at Penguin – specifically Sara Cywinski, Sue Lascelles and Michelle Warner, who made this real and helped me craft this book from the bare bones of an idea to something I am so proud of – thank you!

Chris Sandel, Angela Harkness, Jackie Wren, Lizzie Edwards, Lynn Hord, Miss Lolly, Patty Cruz, Rachel McGuinness and Susie Hasler, all of whom are experts in their fields and people I admire greatly. Thank you for adding your words, wisdom and insights into this book; it's all the richer for your contributions.

Angela Harkness for being the woman I trusted to read my first draft and give me honest feedback. You inspire me to be brave and regularly put 'my big girl pants on'. Thank you.

Cat Townsend who is the reason that all this happened in the first place. Thank you for bringing my dream to life and helping me make a difference in the world.

Mum and Dad, you're the most loving and supportive people I know. You taught me so many life lessons and you inspire me in so many ways. I love you both more than words can ever say.

My amazing family Michael, Auntie Claire, Uncle Ken, Auntie Tina, Uncle Tony, Annie, Lennie, Obi, Churtz, Dan and Nic for always championing and supporting me. I love you all so much.

Danielle, my wing-woman, best friend and soul sister. Even on the other side of the world I know you're right by my side and always will be. Love you long time.

Becky and Jade for backwards high tens, 'How Do I Let Go' moments, letting me know when I need to practise what I preach and for being the rocks I lean on, always. You rock my world.

Steve Walker you changed my life in so many ways and I am forever grateful for the 'Get Mel Plan' and the magic that followed.

My A Team for Bat-Shit-Crazy-Mode and teaching me how to be a better person.

Max Fellows and Courtney Baisch for being the best partners in crime and creating ELEVATE with me.

All the sisters at Sister Snog whose wit, wisdom, support and encouragement is tireless. You are all inspirational and give true meaning to the word 'sisterhood'.

The women I am blessed to call friends who have started businesses and inspire me with their passion to go out and make the world a better place: Amy Thomson, Carol Hanson, Carol Stewart, Carole Bozkurt, Catherine Watkin, Chloe Brotheridge, Emma Lax, Emma Sexton, Deborah Armstrong, Denyse Whillier, Fab Giovanetti, Juls Abernethy, Lauren Arms, Leigh Fergus, Mary Waring, Rebecca Hirst, Sara Ferguson, Samme Allen, Sarah-Jane Baynes,

Rosie Meckliff, Shirley Palmer, Siobhan Costello, Sonia Gill, Susan Heaton Wright and Yifhat Arnstein – you are shining lights for me and so many others.

My teachers at The Animas Institute, The Health Coach Institute and Catherine Watkin from Selling from the Heart. I have grown so much as a result of your training and teaching. Thank you.

My dearest friends who have supported me from day one, you mean the world to me: Eva, Eve D, Eve H, Eryka, Dev, Gloria, Hayley, Honey, Jason, Katy, Luis, David, Sandeep, Sophie, Tal and so many others that I could fill a book naming you all. Know that your friendship is my lighthouse.

My clients who have bared their souls, shared their journey and taught me more than they could ever realise.

Most of all to my husband JP. I couldn't have done this without you and your support. Life wouldn't be half as magical, fun and wonderful without you by my side. Thank you for your unconditional love, support and encouragement – I'd be lost without you.